Disability Awareness
617.481

KU-711-107

Living with Brain Injury

00017899

of related interest

Cracked
Recovering After Traumatic Brain Injury
Lynsey Calderwood
ISBN 1 84310 065 7

Rehabilitation Counselling in Physical
and Mental Health
Edited by Kim Etherington
ISBN 1 85302 968 8

Living with Brain Injury

Philip L. Fairclough

Jessica Kingsley Publishers
London and Philadelphia

All rights reserved. No part of this publication may be reproduced in any material form (including photocopying or storing it in any medium by electronic means and whether or not transiently or incidentally to some other use of this publication) without the written permission of the copyright owner except in accordance with the provisions of the Copyright, Designs and Patents Act 1988 or under the terms of a licence issued by the Copyright Licensing Agency Ltd, 90 Tottenham Court Road, London, England W1P 9HE. Applications for the copyright owner's written permission to reproduce any part of this publication should be addressed to the publisher.
Warning: The doing of an unauthorised act in relation to a copyright work may result in both a civil claim for damages and criminal prosecution.

The right of Philip L. Fairclough to be identified as author of this work has been asserted by him in accordance with the Copyright, Designs and Patents Act 1988.

First published in the United Kingdom in 2002
by Jessica Kingsley Publishers Ltd
116 Pentonville Road
London N1 9JB, England
and
325 Chestnut Street
Philadelphia, PA 19106, USA

www.jkp.com

Copyright © Philip L. Fairclough 2002

Library of Congress Cataloging-in-Publication Data
Fairclough, Philip L., 1951 -
    Living with brain injury / Philip L. Fairclough.
        p. cm.
    Includes bibliographical references and index.
    ISBN 1-84310-059-2 (pbk. : alk. paper)
    1. Fairclough, Philip L., 1951---Health. 2.Brain
damage--Patients--Rehabilitation--Great Britain--Biography. 3. Brain--Wounds and injuries--Complications--Patients--Great Britain--Biography. I. Title.

RC387.5 .F34 2002
617.4'81044'083--dc21

2002016245

British Library Cataloguing in Publication Data
A CIP catalogue record for this book is available from the British Library

ISBN 1 84310 059 2

Printed and Bound in Great Britain
by Athenaeum Press, Gateshead, Tyne and Wear

Contents

I would like to dedicate this book to all those people who helped save my life and helped me and my family regain a reasonable quality of life.

*Devon Air Ambulance,
Derriford Hospital, especially Paul Francel,
Lou Pobereskin and the neurology team,
Torbay Hospital nursing staff,
Rosehill Rehabilitation Unit staff, especially
Penny Weekes and Mandy McVitie.*

And especially to my wife Pauline and our children for sticking by me through the ups and downs of the past seven years and helping and encouraging me with this book.

A BIG THANK YOU

Preface

For most people a journey normally has a destination whatever it may be. It also has a definite time of departure and even then doesn't usually begin without much preparation and expectation. The road to brain injury doesn't have any of these things: it begins unexpectedly, often horrifically and has no known end. How it proceeds, how long it proceeds and where it proceeds to depends on many variables – the type and extent of the injury, the condition and attitude of the victim, the speed of the medical treatment and the help received towards recovery.

My journey down this unknown road began around four o'clock in the afternoon on Monday 7 November 1994 following a work-related accident. When I eventually returned home several months later, despite the excellent help and knowledge gained, I was quite understandably anxious to know more about the results of brain injury, the effects on its victims and their families and how best they all could cope.

With this in mind, therefore, I went to my local library and scoured the healthcare section but only drew a blank. Oh, there were any number of books for myalgic encephalomyelitis (ME) sufferers, for those with multiple sclerosis (MS), cancer or strokes, Alzheimer's and lupus disease and many more ailments besides, but not one dealing with brain injury or anything remotely related. Nor were there any in the library district records.

Considering, as I learned, that every minute at least two people nationwide are admitted to a hospital with some form of head injury (which often results in brain injury), it soon became apparent that a practical help book on the subject could well prove beneficial to many people, nationally and perhaps even internationally.

Knowing I had been interested in writing before my accident, one of the occupational therapists (OTs) at the rehabilitation unit that had cared for me had, on my discharge, suggested I might make the writing of just such a book a project, both as a form of therapy and as a means of helping others. I was further encouraged by Lou Pobereskin, one of the neurosurgeons who operated on me.

So whether you are a sufferer like me, a friend, relative or carer of a sufferer, one of the medical personnel in hospitals or rehabilitation units involved with caring for sufferers or just someone interested in knowing more about brain injury and whether there really is life after brain injury, you possibly have many questions: What can sufferers and carers expect in the short- and the long-term? Can they prepare and if so, how? And, most importantly of all, how can they cope?

With this book, I have tried to answer these and many other questions. It is not a medical or a scientific textbook, neither is it a definitive work, nor does it make any claim to be such. Although much of the information is based on my own personal experience, it is not meant to be autobiographical. Information on such things as Post-Vegetative State (PVS) and alternative medicine is from my own reading and interpretation of research and newspaper reports.

I have written from a patient's perspective with some added insights from my family on what it is like to live with brain injury and I hope to show that contrary to many popular misconceptions, there really is life after brain injury. I hope especially to help carers better understand why a sufferer does, says and acts the way they sometimes do and what in some cases to expect. If this enlightens them, then they will be able to deal better with the situation and the book will have hit the mark I set for it.

Chapter 1

My Introduction to Brain Injury

Before the accident, Dartmouth 1993.

I could say that indirectly my brain injury was caused by Margaret Thatcher and the economic recession of the early 90s but that would be stretching the bounds of credulity somewhat. Since 1978 I had been selling commercial catering equipment and food machinery, the last few years running my own business in the south west of England and turning over somewhere in the region of a quarter of a million pounds annually. Then the recession started to bite and I could see the writing on the wall for many businesses in the food trade. I still had a wife and three children to support and a mortgage to pay, so whilst winding my business down I began to look for a change of direction.

There seemed to be no jobs available that I was qualified for (except selling, for which I was told I was either overqualified or, at 41, too old) so I began looking for work which might be available to me in a self-employed capacity and still provide a decent wage. A friend of mine suggested cleaning windows, particularly in a couple of villages outside Paignton. The inhabitants were a mix of business people, civil servants, artists, people from the forces and everyday people like myself. Certainly, when I began canvassing the area, upon seeing the size of many of the houses and then pricing them up it seemed as if here was the answer to my needs.

Over the next couple of years, through canvassing and referrals, my clientele grew. It almost didn't feel like work to work for such generally pleasant people in such beautiful surroundings down by the River Dart. The last thing on my mind was the danger involved and that it was a high risk business. I suppose that when it became clear that the personal accident insurance premium was financially outside my reach, I should have taken that as a warning; but there we are, hind-sight is a marvellous thing.

However, the days rolled by to that fateful Monday in November 1994. When I looked out the window at 7am that morning, all I could see were grey clouds of drizzle scudding over the town and out to sea. Knowing how capricious the weather could be, I kept my eye on it and a little later it cleared up sufficiently for me to tell my 19-year-old son James, who worked with me, that we might as well get off and see what we could do. So we prepared ourselves for work and by 8.30am were loaded up and ready to go. My memory of the rest of the morning is very vague.

James tells me that we had already completed the morning's work before we moved on to what was to become our last house, Traceys Farm, the home of Russell and Anne Williams. Normally I cleaned this house on my own since Russell was working on the farm and Anne was usually out playing golf or shopping but this day she was home. I do remember James and I eating our lunch in his Morris Ital van and also our starting work, myself as usual on the first floor and James on the ground floor as he wasn't happy with ladders. After cleaning only one or two windows, I moved my ladders round to the front of the house but from then on I have absolutely no recollection of the next two and a half weeks. The rest of the story is now filled in by James, my wife Pauline and the Air Ambulance paramedics.

James says he was watching me from across the patio and thinks my aluminium ladders started to slide on the damp UPVC window bottom. He says that for months after, he relived the horror of the next few minutes as I fell 10 to 15 feet to land head first onto the concrete patio. Then began several coincidences of that day: the first being that James was with me and Anne was home.

James rushed into Anne and between them they notified first the Ambulance Service and then a part-time nurse who lived in the village and was off duty that day. She helped James, who had some first aid training, to keep me comfortable as I was having seizures. Since there were no land ambulances available just then, the Air Ambulance (which didn't normally work on Mondays due to lack of funds) was dispatched and directed to land in the farm paddock on sheets laid out by Anne in the form of a cross. James was, of course, beside himself but when the helicopter arrived they were able to take over.

They laid me in the belly of the aircraft on a stretcher, attached to various monitors. On speaking to the paramedics since then, they tell me that twice during the short flight I went into respiratory arrest and they didn't expect me to survive above an hour after arrival at Derriford Hospital. Both were pleasantly surprised to hear a couple of days later that I had pulled through and was still alive. In Chapter 9, you will read of the sterling work done by Paul Francel and a rather uncertain neurological team. My next recollection was of intense pain in my fingers and nipples and that was my introduction to brain injury.

In 1996, when I visited the National Society for Epilepsy in Gerrards Cross for a magnetic resonance imaging (MRI) scan, the specialist, Dr Duncan, showed Pauline, James and me the x-ray type results of the scan. He pointed out the black areas indicating brain damage and said in a very serious tone, 'According to these plates Mr Fairclough, you shouldn't be here at all, you should be dead!' I am sure you can imagine our feelings at receiving that news but it just goes to show that for someone with a head injury, life does not necessarily automatically end. You may ask, however, just what are the facts regarding brain injury. Let us look more into that subject in the next chapter.

Chapter 2

Brain Injury
The Facts and Some Statistics

The facts

More people now than ever before are aware that the brain is just a few pounds of soft grey matter and works by continuous electrical and chemical processes sending information from one brain cell (of which we are born with 100 billion) to another. When the brain is damaged in some way or other, thought processes and/or motor responses are interrupted or, in some cases, temporarily or permanently disconnected, much the same as when an electrical appliance is separated from its power source.

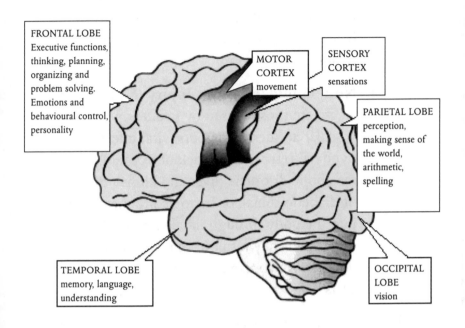

FRONTAL LOBE
Executive functions,
thinking, planning,
organizing and
problem solving.
Emotions and
behavioural control,
personality

MOTOR
CORTEX
movement

SENSORY
CORTEX
sensations

PARIETAL LOBE
perception,
making sense of
the world,
arithmetic,
spelling

TEMPORAL LOBE
memory, language,
understanding

OCCIPITAL
LOBE
vision

Figure 2.1 The brain[1]

Unless a brain injury is congenital or caused by birth trauma, it is classed as an acquired brain injury (ABI) and is caused by an external physical force or by metabolic derangement – that is, an upset in the body's metabolism. ABIs are in turn subdivided into Traumatic and Non-Traumatic.

- **Traumatic Brain Injury** (TBI). These are described as open or closed head injuries such as those caused by accidents (work-related, sport or road) and assaults and involve anything that can damage brain tissue, e.g. skull fracture, shearing, bruising, bleeding, microscopic tearing and lack of oxygen.

- **Non-Traumatic Brain Injury** (NTBI). These are those caused by strokes and other vascular accidents, tumours, viral infections, hypoxia (restriction or lack of oxygen), metabolic disorders (liver and kidney diseases or diabetic coma), or by toxic products taken into the body through inhalation or ingestion. They result in some of the same things that can damage brain tissue as in TBIs.

There are many words and medical terms used in relation to brain injury which may cause confusion, worry or even fear in carers or sufferers – such words as haemorrhage, haematoma and Persistent Vegetative State (PVS).

Haemorrhage is a bleeding within or on the surface of the brain. Haematoma is a collection of blood outside a blood vessel in the brain and can cause two types of problems – it can prevent blood getting to an area of the brain near the clot or it can result in a build up of pressure within the skull leading to damage of vital nerve centres. PVS is often a result of an ABI and is a coma from which there appears to be no hope of recovery. For long periods of time (sometimes running into years) there are minimal responses to external stimuli and many bodily functions are performed by machine. Yet, this is not always true; victims can sometimes breathe independently or may require full-time nursing care for feeding, dressing and washing etc. However, in some rare cases the victims do recover and tell how all the time they were apparently unconscious, they were aware of what was going on around them – especially when they were the subject of discussion – but they could not communicate. They describe their situation as rather like being buried alive.

Often when there is no recovery, after taking medical and legal advice, the family makes the heart-breaking decision to allow their loved one to die with dignity and so agree to the withdrawal of treatment and nutrition. The historic, ground-breaking legal case which first dealt with this matter was in 1993 when the House of Lords ruled that Tony Bland, a victim of the Hillsborough football stadium disaster in 1989, had a right to die and so allowed his parents to cease artificial feeding. This of course raises many other dilemmas and controversies – moral, legal, medical and even religious – but I don't intend to pursue any of these since every case is different and personal to the family.

One other fact that is becoming clearer is the marvellous ability of the brain for self-repair and healing. In

January 2000, the *New York Times* ran an article entitled 'A Decade of Discovery Yields a Shock about the Brain' (4 January 2000). The article discusses the fact that up until the 1990s it was believed that unlike certain animals, the brains of humans did not produce new nerve cells after birth. In other words, we are born with all the brain cells we will ever need in our lives. However, the article cites new research which indicates that premise to be wrong as not only are new nerve cells produced but the brain is actually constantly renewing and repairing itself, especially in that part associated with short-term memory. Other research has also found that in people over the age of 65, learning new skills and interacting with other people seems to encourage the growth of new cells. Perhaps we do get wiser as we get older!

Interestingly, despite having brain damage I had come to a similar conclusion early on after my accident. How? Well, as outlined earlier, damage to the brain causes a breakdown in the neural network, a breaking of the electrical connections. In Chapter 3, I refer to one of the problems I had when getting dressed; I would insist on putting underpants and T-shirts on inside out or back to front. The way the OTs at Rosehill Rehabilitation Unit, where I spent just over a year on a rehabilitation programme, dealt with this was to sit with me daily as I dressed and then constantly remind me how to put my clothes on. The persistent verbal reminders obviously made an impression on my short-term memory because, eventually, getting dressed properly became second nature.

Later, when I became more 'with-it', it was explained to me what happens when the brain is damaged. Looking back on my experiences with getting dressed, I reasoned that what had happened was that constant verbal reminders had forced the memory to work and in so doing, repaired or replaced the damaged synapses, much the same way the body heals itself when it is cut, bruised or injured in some other way. I tried out the veracity of this idea by trying to learn the names of all the Rosehill staff which at that time numbered about 30. In order to do this, wherever I was during the day I would constantly repeat the names in my head and try and put faces to them. Before I finally left Rosehill to come home, one staff member expressed amazement that I could remember all the names. I find that same method is still very useful and feel that concentration and repetition are the keys.

Some statistics

The following data is taken from the Department of Health's website and is based on figures from the NHS Hospital In-Patient Data '1998/99 Key Facts and Figures'. During this period, 125,557 people were diagnosed at NHS hospitals in England as having head injuries (which often result in brain injuries) and of this number 68 per cent were male. Headway, the brain injury association, cite on their website some dated but interesting figures and statistics produced by McMillan and Greenwood (1991). It is estimated that out of every 100,000 of the population:

- between 10 and 15 will suffer severe head injury – this means over six hours of unconsciousness and Post-Traumatic Amnesia (PTA) of over 24 hours (PTA refers to the time between injury and recovery of continuous memory)

- between 15 and 20 will sustain a moderate head injury – involving a loss of consciousness of up to six hours and PTA up to 24 hours – and

- between 250 and 300 will have a mild head injury involving either brief unconsciousness or none at all, with PTA of less than an hour yet appearing apparently uninjured.

From the above data adapted from the Headway website, it is apparent that the potential for brain injury is very high. The 15 to 29-year-old age group is most at risk of head injury and within this group, males are five times more likely to sustain head injuries. Out of every 1000 sustaining head injury in this group, approximately 9 die. This leaves a large proportion of young

TBI survivors and potentially a large number requiring 24 hour medical care. In addition to these figures from Headway (McMillan and Greenwood 1991), according to R. Appleton and T. Baldwin in their book *Management of Brain-Injured Children* (1998), it is estimated that nationwide between 5 and 6 per cent of children under 14 years of age are admitted to hospital with a closed head injury.

Summary

So it becomes readily apparent that many people like me and my family are going to be suddenly thrust into a situation rather like that of a blind man without a guide. It is my hope that this book will prove to be of some benefit as a guide.

Note

1. Figure 2.1 'The brain' is reproduced with permission from *Head Injury – A Practical Guide,* Trevor Powell, Speechmark Publishing/Winslow Press and Headway (1994), and from Headway – the brain injury association.

Chapter 3

The Symptoms

The First Few Days

Diagnosis

As with many injuries and ailments, a reliable and immediate diagnosis of brain injury is not always possible. Even though the cause of the injury is known – as for example in my case a severe head injury – the initial symptoms are no guarantee that brain injury has occurred. Some head injuries never develop beyond being just that, a head injury. So how can one tell the difference?

In most cases, the first indications of brain injury may be:

- paralysis of one body part or even a whole side of the body

- the onset of epileptic seizures, of which there are many types

- difficulties with body coordination, walking and/or speech

- confusion, disorientation and agitation.

Yet even with any or all of these, brain injury is still by no means a certain diagnosis. The first step along the way to reaching a firm conclusion is a computerized axial tomogram scan or CAT scan for short. This is performed by means of a computer linked to a machine which takes pictures of the brain in electronic slices and then reconstitutes them into a complete picture of the brain. Brain damage often shows up as dark patches on the brain. However, even after all that an exact diagnosis, especially of the severity of the damage, may not be possible for some time.

Following my accident and two and a half weeks in a coma, despite exhibiting a small number of the first indications of brain injury I listed above and other symptoms and even having undergone a CAT scan, the diagnosis was not conclusive. After I regained consciousness the best that Paul Francel, one of my neurosurgeons, could tell me and my wife Pauline was: 'You might have brain damage but it still might be two years before we know how serious it is and what it is going to leave you with.'

The reason he was unable or unwilling to give an opinion of the length of recovery and the possible outcome was because every brain injury, like every person, is unique and rates of recovery vary. So few doctors will make a prediction even though the carer and sufferer desperately want some indication.

Conditions associated with brain injury

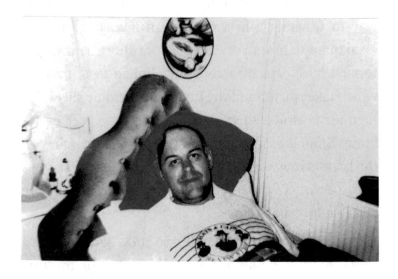

After the accident, at home before the move to Rosehill Rehabilitation Unit. The shape of the skull was caused by the removal of a part of the bone to relieve pressure on the brain.

Among the general public, the picture many have of a victim of brain injury is of someone living in an institution, possibly sitting in a chair or lying down, their limbs flailing about, their eyes rolling, mouth drooling and uttering strange unintelligible noises. Most people's understanding is that such a victim is either destined to a short life or a life permanently in a vegetative state and requiring constant nursing care – in other words their prospects are nil, the hopes of family and friends are pointless, the life of the victim is all but finished.

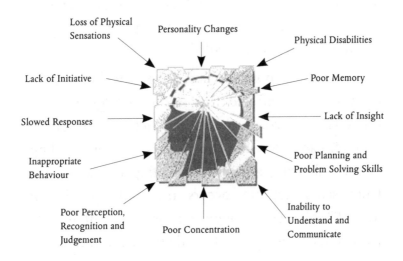

Figure 3.1 The possible outcome of head injury[1]

The purpose of my writing this book is to prove that those views whilst possibly true in a few cases are not true in all. Whilst at Rosehill, the rehabilitation unit I spent just over a year in (from March 1995 to April 1996) after my discharge from hospital, though there were some 30 clients, only two displayed these 'stereo-typical' perceptions of brain injury. The very fact that I am writing this is proof of the reality that the general view is much mistaken.

However, despite all this and after Paul Francel's ominous and negative words, the realities of brain injury began to make themselves apparent. I suppose the first one I was really aware of were the epileptic seizures. As we learned later, there are many types of fitting (as seizures are commonly called).

The ones with which most people are familiar, and from which I suffered first, are called 'grand mals' (tonic-clonic seizures) where the victim often falls (if standing) and goes into convulsions, with eyes rolling, mouth salivating and possible biting of the tongue. Unconsciousness often occurs, the whole thing lasting up to 12 minutes, although this varies according to the patient. Depending on where they are, it can of course be dangerous but death due to seizure itself is very rare.

Perhaps at the other end of the scale of seizures are what I call 'time outs', where the victim suffers a mental blackout for, sometimes, just a few seconds, whilst apparently still conscious. Most frequently, however, it is not until afterwards that they are even aware that anything has happened. But whatever the type, a seizure is generally unpleasant and unpredictable and even though I now only have 'petit mals' perhaps once every seven or eight months (my seizures being controlled by medication), they are something you never really get used to, just learn to live with.

The other major problems associated with brain injury, the understanding of which I did not gain until I was in Rosehill, can be loosely divided into physical (walking, coordination), cognitive (attention, memory, slowed thought processing), executive (planning, judgment – those skills needed to execute a task), psychosocial (personality changes, behaviour, communication). These cover a wide range of difficulties and manifest themselves in a variety of ways but because they overlap in certain areas, I have subdivided them into four main areas: cognitive, perceptual, physical, and emotional and behavioural.

Cognitive

Cognitive symptoms are probably best described as difficulties involving thinking and include problems in processing information – relating what is seen or told to reality and action.

For example, in the early days I would insist on putting certain items of clothing on back to front or inside out or when filling a cereal bowl with milk, I would continue until it poured over the sides. One event which we still laugh about is when I was asked to make a cup of tea for visitors. This was my first time and they all watched as I filled the electric kettle but with insuffi-

33

cient water. It switched off after only a minute or two so I then proceeded to make a drink. When asked whether I had noticed that the kettle had not boiled, my answer was, 'Yes, but I got fed up of waiting because my legs are aching.' Other ways cognitive symptoms manifest themselves are in:

- Maintaining attention to tasks.

- Making decisions.

- Following a set of instructions.

- Shifting attention from one mental task to another, e.g. following a conversation in a crowded room (more in Chapter 9).

- Loss or impairment of memory.

- Language, such as expressing thoughts or understanding what others are saying.

Perceptual

Perceptual symptoms involve problems in interpreting information coming from the senses, such as hearing and vision, and include changes in the five primary body senses. Even now, after seven years, I can some-times have Pauline and the family running around the house looking for something burning because I have smelt smoke. I often smell or taste something which isn't there because my senses have been disrupted.

Another unfortunate and often embarrassing problem in this area is incontinence. The sufferer is not always aware of the evacuation of body fluids – all they know is that they need to go to the toilet, so this may be on the hospital bed or other inconvenient places. Or they simply have no control of the muscles of the bladder or bowels, so whilst they may be aware of the need for the toilet, they are unable to hold on. Whilst this can be embarrassing for the family members, it can at times be very distressing to the sufferer. Other perceptual symptoms are outlined below.

A LOSS OF SENSE OF PERSONAL IDENTITY

'Who am I?' This seemed to happen to me in the early days of my brain injury. I think it was perhaps due to a loss of some of my long-term memory. I didn't really remember much of who or what I was like before the accident. Even now after all these years, I know I sometimes act out of character because my reactions to people and situations don't always feel right or as I would have once reacted, like I know I really am. With help from Pauline and the family I have relearned acceptable social skills but we know and accept that I will never be exactly the same again.

A LOSS OF SENSE OF SPACE

'Where am I and how can I get to somewhere else?' With me, this showed itself early on when walking either inside or out. I would regularly walk into things like doors or door frames etc. When asked why I did it, the best way I could describe it was that it enabled me to determine or judge my position in relation to other objects and space in general. Strange but true!

DISORDERS OF BALANCE

This can cause difficulties and dangers in the early days, for whilst walking up and down stairs I often either missed a step and fell or, whether in or outside, just tripped over things in general. The problem of balance is still with me but is now more of an inconvenience than a danger, causing me at times to stumble into people and things, sometimes tripping over things that aren't even there.

CHANGES IN PAIN SENSITIVITY

For several weeks in hospital, I had the staff baffled by an excruciating pain in my chest and back – they never did find the cause. Generally I sense that I am more sensitive to pain now than I was before the accident.

A LOSS OF SENSE OF TIME

For me this was coupled with a problem in telling the time. At Rosehill, I was in a room of my own, annexed from the main house, so was usually only really aware of what was going on when the OTs came in. I would often wake in the morning, see the daylight, look at my watch and because I was hungry assume it was time to get up. I would then proceed to wash, shave, make my bed and then sit and wait for my breakfast. Many were the times when the night staff would come in after seeing my light on, around three to four in the morning, and ask me what I was doing. I would, with confidence and on occasion petulance, tell them I was waiting for my breakfast.

Physical

Physical symptoms may include the following.

PERSISTENT HEADACHES

These, I suppose, are only to be expected at times following a serious head injury. I had them only occasionally in the beginning, causing me extreme pain, so I was prescribed Ibuprofen daily. However, I found that after I left hospital, apart from an occasional one, the headaches ceased.

FATIGUE

At first, it may seem that all that a victim of brain injury wants to do is rest and sleep, anytime and anywhere. It will eventually become clear, as it did to me, that any physical or mental activity involves the use of the brain and any brain activity tires the body. So even a short walk can be as tiring as a little mental stimulation. Hence the body's energy reserves are soon depleted and need topping up.

This is where the sufferer needs to learn or be taught how to pace themselves, i.e. to learn their limitations and have regular sleep or rest periods (more in Chapter 7). Even now, at times I may feel that to have a sleep during the day is a waste of time when I could be doing other things but eventually I have to give in as the need takes over. After all, sleep is the body's way of healing itself. The *Awake!* magazine, a bi-monthly Jehovah's Witness magazine (8 May 2001, p.28), reports a sleep researcher by the name of Dr James Maas as saying that sleep gives the brain time to restore essential neurotransmitters vital for good memory, prob-lem-solving and learning capabilities. Too little sleep can produce among other symptoms: depression, anxiety and irritability as well as reduced social skills, ability to concentrate and remember, communication and decision-making skills, productivity and general quality of life. Dr Maas concludes, 'We must invest one third of our life in sleep.'

MOVEMENT DISORDERS

These are described as either temporary or permanent spasms, tremors, paralysis or weakness in the muscles. With some it may be no more than a nervous tic but with others it may be an involuntary start or jump in a limb. It is said, by some doctors, that these are minor epileptic seizures which even the normal, healthy body experiences as the body's way of relieving itself of excess electrical energy.

EPILEPTIC SEIZURES

As discussed earlier, these are a usual symptom of brain injury and take many forms depending on the type of injury, the person themselves and their medication. (By adjustments to my dosages of Tegretol Retard and Vigabitrin, my seizure frequency has dropped from one a month to one every seven months with also one period of 13 months and another of 24 months when I didn't experience any seizures.) These same factors will determine the frequency, length and severity of the seizure.

Though some like myself do get what are called auras – a warning that a seizure is due – we still don't know exactly when to expect it. The only sure things about any seizures are their unpredictability, they are never pleasant and there are no known 100 per cent guaranteed cures (not even a very risky surgical procedure with lasers) but they are rarely if ever fatal.

IMPAIRMENT OF FINE MOTOR CONTROLS

Such as picking up small objects.

SENSITIVITY TO LIGHT

SLEEP DISORDERS

I suppose everyone suffers from a sleep disorder at some time in their life, insomnia for example, but my sleep patterns have taken many definite twists and turns in the past seven years. I go from mild bouts of insomnia to my present situation where I waken about 5am and then start dreaming a dream which continues for two to three hours interspersed with periods of wakefulness. Then finally, depending on what time I went to sleep and the activities of the previous day, I will either waken fairly refreshed or absolutely worn out.

SPEECH OR ARTICULATORY DISORDERS

This is probably what leads to many of the mistaken views about brain injury mentioned at the beginning of this chapter; for some, unfortunately, the only sounds they can make do not seem to resemble understandable speech. From my own personal experience at the rehabilitation unit, I would say that only 50 to 60 per cent of victims fit into that category; the rest are quite capable of at least being understood.

Emotional and behavioural

The emotional and behavioural symptoms are possibly what give rise, in my view, to much of the misunderstanding about brain injury.

IRRITABILITY

I have heard women say that when they are beginning, or are due to begin, their period, they can get up in the morning knowing that they are going to be irritable and not be able to do anything about it or about what they might say to loved ones. That description sounds very similar to my experience of irritability in brain injury. Unfortunately for those with epilepsy, one of the side-effects of certain anticonvulsant medication is increased irritability. This condition is really very closely connected to the next.

IMPATIENCE

Someone may say, 'What's so special about that, I'm impatient.' For victims of brain injury, however, impatience may manifest itself in different forms and for different reasons. A person who had before their injury normally been placid and easygoing may now become tetchy and irritated by an apparent slowness in someone else to perform a certain task. They may be impatient over totally trivial, unimportant things.

The causes that create this can perhaps best be explained in the following way. The brain injured person may reason thus, as I often did and still do: 'Why did that person do or not do, say or not say, act or not act in a certain way when they are supposed to be normal? I'm the brain injured one and I wouldn't have dreamt of doing or saying what they did.' The reasoning of suffer-

41

ers is, therefore, sometimes faulty and this shows itself in another way too: when they want something done they seem to want it done then and there, when they want to go somewhere they want to go at that instant, they don't have the patience to wait.

There seem to be two types of faulty reasoning: first, those who are brain injured are ready to get on with whatever the task is at that moment, so they feel that the average person should also be ready; second, the sufferer, who has all the time in the world, has probably been thinking about this matter for some time. So when they decide to ask for it to be performed, they forget that their helper does not have the same amount of free time. As you can imagine this can produce quite a lot of tension, frustration and anger between them. This again is where the patience of the carer can be stretched to the limit.

DEPENDENCE ON OTHERS

Especially in the early days might a sufferer become overdependent on others, either nursing staff or carer. This is often caused by the loss of particular skills and appears to be like reverting to childhood, when they were washed, dressed and fed by their parents and even told when it was time to get up out of bed. Unless proper training is given, the sufferer finds it easier to carry on that way because it takes less mental energy and self-motivation.

DENIAL OF DISABILITY

This could be another sign of faulty reasoning, perhaps due to selective memory loss. If they cannot remember what they were like before the onset of brain injury, how they are now is how they have always been as far as they are concerned and therefore there is nothing wrong with them.

INABILITY TO MANAGE STRESS

The average human body and brain seems to have a built-in pressure valve to cope with or relieve stress and it usually varies from person to person. The sufferer has either forgotten how to cope or quite simply is unable to because that part of the brain is damaged or disconnected. The inability to cope can show itself in a variety of ways, for example in panic attacks – the sufferer being unable to deal with crowds or large groups of people, with loud noise or music. Besides that, for me the inability to cope sometimes manifests itself in the onset of a seizure and therefore I tend to avoid situations which might end in this result. For these reasons, I have turned down several invitations to social gatherings.

Another form of pressure for me can be that either I am unable to grasp something or unable to perform a certain task or am going to do something stressful such as a long car journey or plane flight – just thinking about these things can be stressful even for ordinary people.

APATHY OR LACK OF INITIATIVE

This lack of energy is common in sufferers. For me there were times when, due to a lack of stamina, doing things was just too much effort. Sometimes just trying to work things out in my own head was more trouble than I was prepared to put into it. I do remember saying once that I felt that I was trying to think through cotton wool. I was able to deal with this situation by using the learning skills I was taught at Rosehill, learning to force myself to do things and make decisions, also setting and achieving goals. Pauline continued this arrangement when I returned home and now I do it for myself. There are times when I have to force myself to do something rather than ask someone else to do it.

A LACK OF INHIBITION OR RESTRAINT

This involves not knowing what is proper and accept-able social behaviour. Some usually placid people can become aggressive: shouting, swearing, throwing things and hitting people. Unfortunately, again, some who suffer with epilepsy may find that one of the side-effects of their anticonvulsant medication is an increase in aggression.

Another example of this is unacceptable sexual behaviour. There may be exhibitionism, an inappropri-ate touching of others of the opposite sex or improper conversation with them. Or a sufferer may seem to switch off mentally and rigidly stare at others (especially of the opposite sex) to the point of embarrassment (which I in the past have found myself doing when my mind was on other things).

Another form of unacceptable social behaviour, which although not like any of the above is nonetheless frustrating, is the tendency to interrupt conversations. I think this stems from the sufferer either thinking that what they have to say is more important than what the other person is saying or simply not being interested or losing interest in what the other person has to say. This is also a sign of impatience and faulty thinking which have already been covered. The frequency and serious-ness of this problem is highlighted in the fact that part of my weekly regime at Rosehill was a session on social behaviour. This is something that I still have to work hard to avoid, interrupting the conversations of others when I have something to say which I feel is more important. Pauline still has to nudge me occasionally or give me 'that' look to remind me when I forget.

INABILITY TO CHANGE BEHAVIOUR IN RESPONSE TO ALTERED CIRCUMSTANCES

We might say that in some ways this is a follow on from the previous subject. Sufferers often cannot tell by the body language of others when it is time to hand a con-versation over. Sometimes, a little like children, they become so engrossed in telling a story or being the centre of attention that they cannot tell that the circumstances surrounding them have changed and it's time to be quiet. Even now at times, I find myself being the only one doing the talking and have been for quite some time.

INCREASED OR DECREASED EMOTIONAL RESPONSES

Decreased responses can often be very distressing to loved ones and something the sufferer is not aware of and has to relearn. For example, loving glances, smiles, expressions such as 'I love you', maybe even a kiss, begin to seem rare or non-existent and have to be requested, or the sufferer may just have a fixed stare or expressionless face.

At the other end of the scale, increased responses reveal themselves in a tendency to cry at the least thing. The cause might be a perceived slight from a stranger, an upset with a loved one or friend or a sad scene in a book, television programme or film. Other related emotions include feelings of despondency, despair and hopelessness. This increased sensitivity could perhaps be likened to teeth which are sensitive to hot or cold or to a tender spot somewhere on the skin.

Summary

These conditions are just some but not all of those experienced by victims of brain injury. Some of them are quite obvious to observers but others are less so because, apart from a loved one, often the only other person who is aware of them is the sufferer. All of this has led the medical profession and others to call brain injury the 'Hidden Disability'.

I have suffered from and still suffer from some of the symptoms and the information recorded here is based on many of my own personal experiences, but this is not to say that everyone has or will suffer from all or even some of them – everyone is different and so their experiences will differ.

Note

1. Figure 3.1 'The possible outcome of head injury' is reproduced with permission from *Head Injury – A Practical Guide*, Trevor Powell, Speechmark Publishing/Winslow Press and Headway (1994), and from Headway – the brain injury association.

Chapter 4

Coping with Your Feelings

Accepting and digesting the news

Consider the following scenario: you go to sleep one night and when you wake up the following day, you are in a strange place surrounded by people you don't know. One of them comes over to you and says, 'I'm sorry to tell you but you have an incurable cancer.' After the initial shock and panic goes away you think, 'Hang on a minute. Even though I am in hospital, I feel fine and look OK as far as I can see and I was alright when I went to sleep. There must be some kind of mistake, they've made an error and they think I'm somebody else.' Then you relax and maybe laugh, 'Yes that's it, either that or this is just one very realistic bad dream.' But eventually, when your family come to see you and ask how you are feeling, you notice you've been operated on and as a nurse comes to take your pulse and temperature, you realize it's very real and then freak out.

Over-dramatized? Not really, this is how brain injury strikes some people, depending of course on the type of injury. For some who suffer an aneurism (burst blood vessel) or a subdural haematoma, the above scenario is only too real. Very likely, the last thing they remember is lying in bed or performing some task. For those like me who suffer a head injury, the last thing they may remember is being at work, crossing a road, driving a car, enjoying a sport or even just walking down the road but, fortunately for them, the brain does not want to remember the next bit so selective amnesia kicks in. The next things of which any of them are aware and which are only too painfully obvious are probably bandages on their head, finding themselves connected to a drip of some sort or, as in my case, a life support machine, with nurses running around and their spouse sitting holding their hand.

As you can imagine, for anyone to wake up to that would be quite startling and take some swallowing. Unfortunately, the above scenario is only too real in the cases of some victims. They are unable to grasp the full extent and seriousness of their situation. In fact some never do, living as some doctors say in denial, the brain unable or unwilling to accept the situation. For those who can and do accept their state, however resignedly, they all have to contend with some or all of the following emotions.

Anger, frustration and resentment

Anyone reading this who is not familiar with brain injury may at first find it strange that a sufferer should feel any of the above emotions or others we shall discuss later. Let me explain.

Whether the sufferer was a window cleaner, rock climber, driver or pedestrian the *anger* can be directed at, among others, any one of the following: him or herself for not being more careful; the manufacturer of the equipment being used; the dangerous driving of the other driver or the lack of care of the pedestrians; or maybe the police for not making the streets in that particular locality safer for law-abiding citizens to walk down. As can be seen, the anger is very likely to be aimed at other people, mostly anyone other than themselves, even if it was quite simply an accident.

The *frustration* is an unusual emotion and is often a result of hindsight – the 'What if?' syndrome. With any of the above situations, the frustration comes basically from the sufferer wishing that they could turn the clock back and change things, that they'd been more careful and aware of others or that they'd known it was so dangerous on the streets of that certain area of town.

Resentment is really a symptom of the 'Why me?' syndrome. The sufferer sees other people moving around the ward, nurses, doctors and visitors, and thinks, 'Why did it have to happen to me? What did I ever do to anyone?' Or they may even look at someone else with a brain injury but who is not so badly damaged and have the same thoughts. Of all the emotions they may feel, this is probably the most selfish. What they are in effect saying is, 'Why didn't it happen to someone else instead of me?' But if they are really honest with themselves, would they truly want anyone else to go through what they have gone through? I don't think many truly would.

Under cold analysis it may be felt that, really, all these emotions are pointless and fruitless but that won't stop sufferers from feeling them. In fact the medical profession accepts them as being part of the grieving process it is essential for sufferers to go through before they can move on. They are also possibly the brain's way of relieving a buildup of mental pressure. However, if it can be said that any emotions are understandable and reasonable in sufferers, it is the following three.

Anxiety, worthlessness and the loss of role in life

Whilst *anxiety* may come from a variety of sources, the two main ones are: if the sufferer has been a breadwinner, how will the family cope? Or if the sufferer is a carer for a family member or an ageing parent, who will look after them now? Both are quite reasonable and if anyone else were in these situations, we would expect them to feel the same.

The sufferer may also be anxious if they were responsible for the family accounts or were in the middle of a building or decorating project at home or of a job for a customer. If they are self-employed, maybe they have work lined up so will naturally be anxious about how it will now be accomplished. If they are employed, they will possibly be wondering what will happen to their job. All of these situations can bring on the second emotion.

If anyone has been ill in bed for a prolonged period of time, if only with a bad bout of flu or gastroenteritis, then they know how fretful one can get, just lying there thinking of all the things they could and should be doing. Doesn't it make one feel useless? With brain injury, the feeling of uselessness can grow into a feeling of *worthlessness*.

The sufferer feels of no value to anyone, they think: 'I am now of no use to my family, I'm just a burden to them, I'll never be able to do anything worthwhile for them ever again.' The lack of self-worth develops into a lack of self-confidence and so depression can easily set in. The sufferer just sees themselves as a lump of flesh laid on a bed whilst everyone else runs around looking after them. This feeling of worthlessness is related to the sense of *a loss of role in life*.

For me this was, and still is, the loss of my role as the principal breadwinner in my family. Like many sufferers I felt I would probably never work again and that my position as provider and protector of my family was lost to me. This feeling can be further accentuated for a sufferer if one's partner now has to go out to work or the family has to survive on government benefits. This loss of role has been described by some as producing a feeling of grief, rather like one would mourn over a dead family member or friend.

Dealing with overprotectiveness

When a person is brain injured, either they become overprotective of themselves or their carer becomes overprotective of them. Usually the neurosurgeon and medical staff will have stressed to the sufferer and their family or the carer just how delicate the brain and skull now is: rather like when new parents first find out that babies after birth have a soft spot on the head which must always be protected.

So the brain injured must protect their heads at all costs, for even a slight knock or bang on the head can produce a haematoma or blood clot. The effects of this can range from the serious to a temporary partial paralysis or to nothing at all – a clot may just sit there until it is reabsorbed. Unless it is dangerous not to, surgeons are loathe to open up the skull too many times. We can therefore see how this situation of overprotectiveness may arise and if the carer becomes overprotective, then so may the sufferer. Wise carers and sufferers take precautions (more on this in Chapter 10).

Taking stock – How much recovery can be made?

It becomes clear from all this that in the early days, after even only a tentative diagnosis is made, the sufferer is going to go through many things. Not only will they feel unwell and be in pain but they will be on an emotional roller coaster, feeling very confused and worried.

Probably one of their biggest worries is, 'How much recovery will it be possible for me to make?' Perhaps they have seen the results of brain injury in others and have already formed their own opinion or have heard the views of others – that their chances of life and quality of life are poor. There is no straight answer to the question of how much recovery one can make. Unfortunately at this stage in the game, nobody knows or will know for quite some time to come because everyone is different and so the end result cannot be known or predicted by making a comparison with someone else.

The real answer may depend on any one or all of three determining factors: the type of help they receive, what they do to help themselves and their own attitude and frame of mind. I shall be covering these as we go through the rest of the book. The encouraging fact is that most progress is usually made in the first two years after injury, though improvement can continue through life and that is the hope that the sufferer, family and carer must cling to.

What the sufferer and family must accept is that many things will probably never be the same again. The sufferer may still look the same but they will not act as they did before their injury and their relationships will be different too. But none of this gives any of them a reason to mentally lie down, curl up and die. It may be the end of one road but the beginning of a new one.

No one must become negative and give up hope. My motto from the beginning has been, 'Where there is life there is hope.' Part of how much recovery a victim of brain injury makes can be attributed to the team effort but can also begin even whilst the sufferer is still in care. I think a positive attitude is the key, even in the face of long-term problems.

Chapter 5

Home Care or Care Unit?
The Big Dilemma

The question of whether to bring a loved one who is a sufferer back home to live or to place them in a special care unit may seem to some reading this callous and unfeeling. A carer with a loved one who is a sufferer may feel that the question would never arise. Emotional and difficult though this issue may be to face, nonetheless it must be faced realistically. As one who is a sufferer and has been in a special care unit, I raise this point for several good reasons but I stress that we need to remember that every individual and situation is different and this will have a bearing on the issue.

Since the sufferer may well be as we say 'out of it', the weight of making this serious decision will fall mostly on the shoulders of the carer with help from the medical team. The very fact that the question might arise may depend much on two matters: first, the seriousness of the injury, the abilities or lack of on the part of the sufferer and the long-term prognosis, i.e. whether it is thought they are ready to go home and even whether it is felt they will get the help they need; and, second, whether the carer wants them home and whether they feel they can cope physically, mentally, emotionally and maybe even financially.

Before we get to considering these points in depth we need to first lay a foundation: that it is true to say that all victims of brain injury, regardless of the cause, will begin their treatment in hospital. Unfortunately, however, not every hospital is geared to dealing with brain injury. For example, I was first taken to Derriford Hospital in Plymouth which had a neurology department, since the hospital nearer to my home didn't (at the time). I was eventually discharged three weeks later from Derriford, which is almost 30 miles from my home, to be nearer my family. Upon arrival at the nearer hospital in Torbay, I was first placed in an asthma ward – I'm not sure if this was because they didn't have anywhere else to place me or simply because that was the intake ward for the day. Then I was transferred to a stroke ward because the symptoms of stroke victims are often similar to those of brain injury. I must say they did their best to help me despite their limited resources.

Since I had lost the use of my left side, my mobility was severely reduced and I was very unsteady, causing me to either stumble or drag my left leg, so the main help I was given was by the physiotherapy department. They continued with the course of physiotherapy that had been started at Derriford and daily, with a therapist on either side of me for support, I would walk back and forth in the ward. This helped strengthen my left leg so that as far as I recall, by the time I left hospital five weeks after the accident, I was more or less mobile. They had also helped me with my balance through the use of very large balls which I had to lie across and propel myself along. They also helped me with cookery. I cooked my first chips, since the accident, in the physiotherapy department kitchen and nearly set the place alight but we survived.

Reflecting on my time there has since led me to feel that certain hospitals are either just not geared for the long-term care of the brain injured and their special needs, or simply that they are so overstretched that they may need to devote more time to people who are acutely ill. This, I feel, is where the rehabilitation units come into their own – they have long-term specialists in occupational, speech and physiotherapy whereas some hospitals can only deal with clients on a short-term basis.

The unit I was referred to was Rosehill in Torquay because they had a contract with the Health Authority to take on clients with brain injury. I arrived at Rosehill almost five months after my accident. When I was there, there were 30 clients each with their own rooms. We all ate together, could meet up in the common room and, whilst I was there, I was visited daily. At Rosehill they did not just put me on a healthcare regime they had running for every other client but, as we shall see, they were able to offer me what I personally needed.

At Rosehill, May 1995, with reshaped skull.

However, before I was accepted there, Pauline and I were invited to a meeting with various members of the specialist team as well as representatives of the social services. The purpose of the meeting was for them to ascertain my needs and those of my family. Once they were armed with that information and I had looked around the unit (Pauline had been before) it was agreed that I would join them a week later, by which time they had produced a prepared weekly schedule tailored to my own personal needs. As I later learned, every client was different and their schedules differed accordingly.

I still have my original first schedule which shows the allowance made for every session with each therapist associated with my personal problems, e.g. social behaviour, relearning time telling, relaxation, stress management and physiotherapy to help me with walking, posture and muscle tone. Every day there was a morning programme to rehearse daily living skills.

I see from subsequent timetables, which I also still have, that as my needs changed so did the sessions. For example, eventually cookery and woodwork skills were added to my ongoing cognitive skills retraining when I felt ready to take them on and other disciplines were either decreased, cut down or dropped altogether as I improved.

Since many people have the mistaken impression that patients in mental health units sit around all day doing things like basket weaving, let me describe a normal week at Rosehill to show the purpose and aims of each session and their achievements. This may even help a would-be carer make an informed decision if they are unsure of what to do for the sufferer.

On most days there was a group physiotherapy session from 10am to 11am. For me, the timing was just right since then as now, partly due to my stamina levels and partly the results of my anticonvulsant medication, I am not up to much before 9.30am. The half-hourly sessions were made up of various exercises designed to help us with balance, coordination and stamina.

One thing particularly watched for was something common to brain injured people that was laughingly called the 'handbag hand'. When there has been paralysis on one side, the hand on that side may often be held up near the chest rather like a woman holding a handbag. It was almost as if our brain would not allow us to just let the arm hang by our sides. With exercise and constant reminders we learned to let that hand hang naturally by our side. I must say however that even after all these years there are odd occasions when I find my left hand feels almost uncomfortable to hang down and I have to force myself to let go.

I see on the schedule that there were rest periods morning and afternoon. Although we might not actually sleep at these times, their main purpose was to help us learn to relax and rest our bodies when they needed it, to get into the habit of taking time out to allow the brain and body to rest. Even now, though at times I find it frustrating, if I am in the middle of doing something, I occasionally have to have an afternoon nap because I find I just cannot keep going. The walk with a physiotherapist was an individual thing. In my case, its purpose was to help me with stamina levels. To begin with, a short walk was all I could cope with but upon finally leaving the unit a year later, I was able to walk for around half to three- quarters of a mile.

The group sessions with Penny and Mandy, two of the OTs, started almost as soon as I arrived and were designed to help several of us relearn our social skills within a group setting – how to take turns in conversation, for example. We were also videoed as we went through this so we could later watch ourselves and look for areas of improvement. Other skills we had to relearn were anxiety and anger management, and also memory testing. These, along with certain cognitive skills, were worked on by playing such group games as Jenga. This, for the uninitiated, is a tower made up of interlocking wooden blocks which have to be removed and placed elsewhere on the tower without causing it to collapse. This was a great help in relearning balance, coordination and perception as well as interacting and relating with others.

Our group session with therapist Andy related to woodwork and involved designing an object for use in the home, then planning and working to its completion, all of course under supervision. The first thing I made was a display case for my son Jordan's model vintage car collection. We all also had several individual sessions with different therapists, depending on our personal needs. For example, my cookery session in the special kitchen for clients required that I first plan at home a main course for my family, then bring along the ingredients, cook the meal under supervision and then take it home, still warm. The main things this taught me were timekeeping, accuracy in weights and safety in the kitchen. One of the most amusing sessions I used to have was with Caroline Harlowe, the speech therapist. With her I relearned time telling by means of an Early Learning clock and she also had to listen to me as I tried once again to sing in key.

Rehabilitation units are, in my opinion, a very necessary halfway house for support, understanding and retraining of sufferers and their families. Whilst hospitals are vital in the treatment of brain injury they may be limited in what they can do long-term for victims of TBI. However, I cannot diminish the hospital staff's professionalism and their depth of care and understanding.

Whether a rehabilitation unit becomes a permanent home for the sufferer or they return home depends much on the matters I raised earlier so let me deal with them one at a time. The seriousness of the injury, the abilities or lack of on the part of the sufferer and the long-term prognosis may necessitate them remaining in an environment which is specially made to help and care for them, e.g. special beds, toilets or just simple movement around. Some carers may say they would have their home adjusted to meet such needs – wheel-chair ramps, bannisters and hand rails, stair lifts and even a downstairs toilet.

This course should, I feel, never be discouraged. However, the rehabilitation unit may, before encouraging this course, consider whether in their opinion the sufferer is ready to go home or needs further retraining in the areas mentioned above, and also whether they will receive the help they need from the carer.

Caring for a sufferer of brain injury can be a 24 hour occupation, especially in the early days. The rehabilitation unit will take into consideration the age and health of the carer – whether they are a young or old person, fit or infirm. So whilst a carer may want to have a loved one at home with them because they love them, or they feel they have a moral responsibility or maybe because of the stigma or connotation that the word 'institution' carries, many serious matters must be considered before the decision is made.

One other consideration is, does the carer want the sufferer home? Again it may be questioned that this would surely never happen, that someone would not want a loved one at home rather than in an institution or home. There could unfortunately be any number of reasons why this might be. The simplest may be the misconception of what brain injury is. To have at home and care for someone who is inarticulate, unintelligible and has no mobility or control over their bodily functions is more than some people can cope with, no matter how much they love them. Pauline says that when she first saw me in hospital, battered, bruised and unconscious, and was told she would be taking this stranger home to care for, she nearly freaked out and it took her a while to come to terms with the situation.

Even if the carer has all the facts and knows what is involved in caring for a sufferer, they may feel that they just can't cope. They may have already, as many have in this day and age, had to care for an elderly relative, perhaps watching them deteriorate into dementia, then death, and they just don't feel they can cope with all that again.

And finally, the sufferer may not have been a very pleasant person as a husband, wife or parent and the carer quite simply doesn't want them back to try and care for someone who is possibly worse than before. I said at the outset that this is a difficult and emotional subject. When I first raised this with Pauline several years ago and she said she understood why some carers left a sufferer in a care unit, I thought she was being hard and I didn't understand. However, she then explained the above points to me and I saw it from a different angle. I hope that if the same thing happened to her or our children that I would have the same love, care, strength and devotion she has shown to me.

But I also hope that anyone reading this who has either had to make or has yet to make this very difficult decision will find this viewpoint sensitive and helpful. I advise them to weigh up all the facts, take the advice of the rehabilitation unit and try to be guided by the mind as well as the heart. If the reader knows someone who has had to make this decision, I would say don't judge them. I hope those faced with this decision, armed now with this advice, consider realistically how to cope if presented with the 'Big Dilemma' – home care or care unit?

Chapter 6

The First Few Weeks

From the Rehabilitation Unit to Home

Whilst still in care, whether that be in a hospital that is geared towards neurology or a rehab unit, there are four main areas that are worked on with the sufferer which are vital if they are to obtain any quality of life when they return home: communication, mobility, eating, and dress and grooming. Depending on the practitioners available – the physiotherapists or occupational therapists – one area or several may be covered at one time. The main factor governing which regime is followed may be simply the needs of the individual and their capabilities. When the sufferer returns home, the carer will be advised which methods to use in dealing with these four main areas of life but they will probably also develop their own system with time and practice.

Communication

The level of help that needs to be given in this area depends to a great degree on the type of brain injury suffered. In a stroke type of injury, there may be either a slight or total speech impairment or, as in my type of injury, speech may be hardly affected except for a little slowness or slurring of words. If the communication problem is one of speech, this is where speech therapists come into their own and as can be imagined, to teach someone to speak again is a challenge. Before I deal with that, let me tell you of another challenge which my speech therapist faced.

Following the accident I had a problem with singing. I was unable to cope with musical notes and tones, caused partly by damage to the area of the brain controlling the vocal chords (though whether I could sing properly before the accident is debatable!). My speech therapist had to teach me to relearn the forming of sounds by shaping the mouth and humming. I did this along with music that I already knew. With practice, I regained some of my ability but still can only sing a song provided it begins on the C chord, so Pavarotti can rest easy!

For some of those whose speech control is totally impaired, they may have to communicate by means of a keyboard and screen rather like a computer. However, with sufferers such as those with PVS, communication may only be possible by pressing a buzzer, one for yes and two for no etc. Whilst communicating may be difficult for some, it is vital to have some form of communication with all sufferers in order to know their requirements or problems. If the sufferer is having difficulty making themselves understood, it will be very frustrating for them so the carers will need to exercise a great deal of patience and understanding. With time they may be able to establish some form of communication that they both at least understand.

We have friends who have a son aged nearly 24, who has cerebral palsy. Even though he now uses a keyboard to communicate, in the early days only his brother and parents seemed to understand the noises he made but it was his way of communicating. So if communication is a problem, stick with it even if it is only by means of messages written on notepaper. It is vital to all concerned.

Mobility

This is also vital, if possible, but at first a wheelchair or stick may be necessary. Carers will probably be advised to pursue the same regimen as has been used in the hospital or rehab unit. Much of the training in mobility is dealt with in physiotherapy. When one of the first symptoms of brain injury is a paralysis of some part of the body, mobility can be a real problem and may manifest itself in a variety of ways.

Since the left-hand side of the brain controls the right side of the body and vice versa, depending on which side of the brain the injury is, either total or partial paralysis of that corresponding side of the body may occur. It can be similar to when someone suffers a stroke: the leg may become totally immobile or may drag whilst walking. In brain injury I found that the use of the leg can be improved by various exercises such as standing and holding onto a firm chair back, table top or even a kitchen work surface, then by swinging the leg forwards, backwards and side to side. Another method is to lie on one's back and slowly raise and lower the leg. All of this involves a movement of the hips.

The same type of exercises can be used irrespective of which part of the body is in trouble. Of course, what is really happening with any exercise is not only a strengthening of the limb but, perhaps more importantly, a reteaching of the brain on how to use the limb, i.e. the making of new neural connections to replace damaged or broken ones.

Once the sufferer has gained the strength and confidence to use the leg, the next stage is to begin to use it in climbing up and then stepping on and off the bottom two or three steps of a flight of stairs. Then they can begin walking, at first short distances and then increasing the distance as progress is made. Maybe like me they will never get back to fell walking, climbing ladders or going for long hikes but the independence which comes from being able to go out without the need of a wheelchair, walking stick or even a companion is immeasurable. A sufferer of brain injury need not be tied to a chair or bed.

As already noted, the lack of mobility may be caused by paralysis on one side or the other. This may bring with it a loss of use of the arm and/or hand on that side. How can this be dealt with? The physiotherapists will no doubt first set in place a series of daily exercises for the arm: raising, lowering and swinging it by holding it and then showing the patient how to do it. Their main aims are to prevent the muscles from becoming flabby through lack of use, to build up muscle tone and to help the brain get used to using the arm once again.

Once they have got this regime going, the occupational therapists will then add their contribution by installing daily exercises to strengthen the use of the hand. There are a number of ways of doing this: by bringing the fingers back to the palm of the hand one at a time or by continually moulding and remoulding plasticine or play dough in the hand or rolling it around in a ball on a table top. It is surprising how much versatility this gives to the hand, thus enabling one to go on to learn how to pick up small objects. This then enables the patient to go back to the physiotherapists for training in picking up and throwing balls etc. These exercises are something carers can do once the sufferer is back home, they can carry on where the rehabilitation left off.

This is not meant to sound simplistic or as if to suggest that overcoming paralysis is a walkover. It is not; when I first arrived at Rosehill in March 1995 I could only stand for eight minutes unaided and it was not until the end of the year that I stopped using a wheel-chair to go out from home. As you can see it may take several weeks or even months before some real progress is made and with some it might not happen at all – but if it is never started, nothing will ever happen.

Eating

Problems with eating may be a result of a cognitive difficulty and/or a perceptual problem (see Chapter 3). The sufferer is unable to gauge distances and height, leading in some cases to an inability to keep food on the spoon or fork or to get it safely to the mouth. This can lead to much frustration on the part of the sufferer and a lot of extra work on the part of the carer who has to clean up the resultant spillages.

In these cases, it would be very easy to resort to spoon-feeding but that would be a retrograde step. There are two reasons for saying this: first, no matter how little it is thought that sufferers understand, they know when they are being treated like a child so resent it and this can distance them from the carer; second, whether that proves true or not, doing so will make it harder to progress – just like spoon-feeding a child means it will take longer before they learn to use a knife and fork properly.

No matter what their relationship is to the sufferer, though a carer must never treat them as a child, they must remember that in a sense that is what they are faced with. They may be presented with an adult but the adult has the attitudes and abilities of a child so a great deal of patience and understanding will be needed. It will help if parents recall how they first taught their small children to eat properly and work accordingly.

Dress and grooming

The same principles apply as with eating. Parents will no doubt remember preparing their children to go out – washing hands and face, brushing hair and straightening clothes. To begin with, it may seem that way all over again if their grown-up son or daughter is the sufferer. But generally, just as when they were small, they learn even though their parents have to keep going back over things.

I suppose those parts of dress and grooming are the easiest to deal with: it gets difficult when it comes to the more intimate or personal matters, e.g. when girls and women have their periods and when men and boys are shaving. As far as menstruation is concerned I cannot, of course, speak with any experience but that is where the OTs will be invaluable. There is nothing they have not had to deal with, so seek their help.

Shaving I can speak on from experience. The OTs in hospital were quite surprised that I could shave myself straightaway, though at the time of course I didn't understand why they were so surprised. However, knowing as I do now that sufferers have problems with perception, trying to shave yourself on one side of the face with the opposite hand must be quite a challenge after brain injury.

Summary

The first few weeks after the return home of the sufferer can be very difficult for them and traumatic for the family. It is difficult for the sufferer because, depending on the seriousness of their injury, they have probably got used to the regime of life in the hospital or rehabilitation unit and are now presented with a new one. It is traumatic for the family because no matter how much they love the sufferer, they have been given their worst nightmare, a stranger or a grown-up child. My wife said for her it was like her husband went out one day and came back a few weeks later as a complete stranger who she had to care for, feed and try to love as her husband.

Well that's the negative side of things, now let us look at the positive side. From all that we have seen so far, the knowledge and ability to do many things has not necessarily been wiped out forever from the brain and memory of the sufferer. It has perhaps just been temporarily misplaced and sits somewhere in the sub-conscious – the task of the carer is to patiently try to help the sufferer rebuild the neural networks and find the misplaced information.

Some may feel I am oversimplifying this but I am writing, I feel, as one who knows and I am certainly not a one in a million case. But if when the sufferer returns home the carer throws up their arms in despair, they will be of no use to anyone. However hard they try they may not be able to help rebuild the neural networks but if they don't try they will never know. I hope this chapter will encourage them to give it their best shot. The first few weeks are just the beginning, there are many long-term problems that sufferer and carer alike will need to understand before they can come to terms with them. The next chapter will deal with some of the major ones.

Chapter 7
Long-Term Problems

So far we have really only looked at the early days of brain injury but now let us look at some of the long-term problems, since before sufferers and carers can deal with their situation, they need to know and understand what they may expect. Let us deal first with some of the changes that might occur in the sufferer.

Psychological changes

When psychological changes are spoken of in relation to people with brain injury, some people automatically think of mental illness, schizophrenia, aggression, reversion to childhood and idiocy among others. Whilst some of these may apply to just a few sufferers, by far the greater number will experience some personality changes with regard to their dealings with other people, e.g. irritability, agitation (restlessness), nervousness (panic attacks), aggression, depression, mood swings and oversensitivity.

In saying that the majority experience more of the above, this is not to say that all will suffer from them in the same way. Again there are many determining factors such as which part of the brain is damaged, what type of medication is being taken, e.g. anticonvulsants, or even the environment in which they are living. I intend therefore to cover the more common ones. That is not to say that the others are not important but I have no experience of them and they are for the most part best dealt with by experts in those fields.

Aggression

Aggression can be shown either physically or verbally – whichever way, it is usually the very opposite of that person's normal personality traits. In my year at Rosehill, I heard a small, inoffensive woman use the foulest invective and I saw physical aggression displayed twice by others. I mention these cases not to cause worry but to illustrate my earlier comments about environment. If each of those people had been at home or somewhere else, those situations would possibly never have arisen since the other person concerned would not have been there to 'push their button', so to speak. However, carers need to be prepared, for someone else might be a trigger.

Carers, especially family, need to remember two things: they must not take aggression personally since they are rarely the cause and the sufferer can't help it and is often very sorry, sometimes giving way to tears of remorse. I feel, looking back on my own situation, that such aggression is not because the sufferer has a short fuse but because of irritability. So let us look at that next.

Irritability

Irritability is something that many people suffer from for a variety of reasons but brain injured people in par-ticular may be often irritated because of frustration and this is not the same frustration as I mentioned in Chapter 4. The frustration is a result of one of the problems of cognitive functioning (see Chapter 3). The sufferer receives information but is unable to process it or they are given instructions and don't understand what to do. Even when something is explained more than once it still doesn't register, so frustration sets in and irritability follows.

And it is not as if they don't want to do something: they simply can't because they either don't understand or can't remember how to do it. They know they should know and should be able to remember but are just totally unable to do so; rather like someone trying to understand something being said by a person in a com-pletely different language.

Nervousness or agitation

This is perhaps a symptom of an inability to manage stress. Before I sustained brain injury, I often stood and gave talks to audiences of around 150 people whom I knew personally, yet after the accident I was unable to even enter the same building with the same people. I suffered from panic attacks which are defined as being the body's response to stressful situations.

Panic attacks also thrive on low self-esteem or lack of confidence and is something that strikes many sufferers of brain injury. I have deliberately not gone into detail in explaining panic attacks but highlight them as just one symptom of nervousness and to stress that they should not be ignored.

Another sign of nervousness or agitation might be the sufferer's apparent inability to sit still, either fidgeting with their hands, feet or whole body. It is hard to understand why they feel stressful in the company of even their own family but of strangers it is perhaps more understandable.

Mood swings

People of both sexes and all age groups are familiar with this condition, especially teenagers in puberty. It can be a difficult time for them and the people around them and it affects sufferers of brain injury in much the same way. They may wake up feeling fine and pleasant but

79

within a few hours, if not by the end of the day, they are miserable, grumpy or depressed, with conversation almost becoming a chore.

This swing between euphoria and depression is another emotional and behavioural problem (Chapter 3) and can be as hard for the carer to deal with as it is for parents of teenagers in puberty. In all these cases the person has very little control over their own emotions. The reasons for euphoria are difficult to understand but depression is a little easier. As already discussed, with brain injury the sufferer may feel that their life has ended and no longer has a purpose – I shall deal further with this in Chapters 8 and 9.

Oversensitivity

Oversensitivity to other people or a persecution complex – such a description may seem a little over-strong in describing sufferers of brain injury but in my experience fits – is another psychological change in brain injury. However, some but not all do develop an attitude of 'they don't like me' about people they come into contact with, even on occasion friends. I know this to be true for I still sometimes have this problem.

The causes may be related to the sufferer's loss of confidence or self-esteem. Because they feel less of a person due to their injury, a look, comment or gesture is sometimes perceived as a put-down by the other person.

So they feel that they are being left out of a conversation, that they are being treated as invisible or that what they have to say is either unimportant or ridiculous. All of this can have the effect of alienating either themselves or others. This is very unfortunate because outside the family most people don't understand what is going on and so tend to avoid the sufferer, beyond being civil.

This is all often because of the problems discussed in Chapter 3, the disruption to mental functioning brain injury causes, and is saddest when it occurs in people who, to all intents and purposes, appear to be like everyone else. Sadly, because this is often all that outsiders see, brain injury is often called the 'Hidden Disability'. This is the problem I have because physically I don't appear to have anything wrong with me. Pauline says, without malice, that I'm a great con artist since I carry off my condition well. I appear to be just like I used to be since I am determined not to appear different.

This is why it is said that to really understand brain injury, you need to live with a sufferer. So if ever someone feels slighted by a brain injured person, they shouldn't take it personally; the sufferer has probably misinterpreted some sign given by the other person, either verbally or physically. And remember, they are having as much difficulty dealing with their situation as everyone else is.

Sexual difficulties

Whoever said that sex was like riding a bike – you never forget how to do it – had obviously never heard of the problems of brain injury. At the outset, I must stress that since I am not a sex therapist, I do not intend to discuss all the problems and solutions of the brain injured but I will at least highlight just what some of the problems may be.

It is difficult to say whether the inability to perform sexually is the result of an impairment of the memory or the emotions controlling sexual arousal. Whichever it is, in women this seems to cause a loss of libido and in men, impotence. Other problems seem to be either an overexaggerated sexual interest, shown perhaps by inappropriate sexual behaviour (as discussed in Chapter 3), or a total lack of interest in sex.

I have read the results of several studies here and abroad (particularly M. Kreuter *et al.* [1998] 'Sexual Adjustment and Its Predictors after Traumatic Brain Injury') which deal with the brain injured and their sexual situation and several interesting facts emerge. Whilst sexual difficulties may be related to changes in the central nervous system or possibly the results of using anticonvulsant drugs, alternatively they may be caused by a deterioration in the relationships with their spouses. By this the researchers mean, for example, that husbands or wives often feel less affectionate to their brain injured spouses because perhaps they feel they are having sex with a total stranger. Pauline says she can understand that 'in principle'.

She has said that when I first came out of the coma, she felt like screaming when told she could now take me home to care for me, since in some senses I was no longer like her husband: physically, mentally and emotionally I was, at that time, a stranger. However, with the help I was given and her original feelings for me and a sense of responsibility, she gradually learned to cope. Yet with others, without those feelings, a sexless union may develop where neither partner is interested in or feels the need for sex.

So, briefly, these are just some of the psychological changes but fortunately, as with so many areas of difficulty in life, there is an organization that deals with this one – The Association to Aid the Sexual and Personal Relationships of People with a Disability (SPOD). I will cover this more in Chapter 11.

Fatigue and loss of strength

This is probably one of the most frustrating effects noticeable to brain injury victims who regain their mental faculties: the inability to perform what used to be the simplest, normal and in some cases enjoyable activities. Every second of every day unbeknown to us our brain is busy working, running all the body systems we take for granted, e.g. circulation, breathing etc.

However, when the brain is damaged it is unable to continue to supply the energy the body needs for the normal tasks it is asked to perform and the brain is having to work harder just to make simple decisions. This could result in reduced motivation which might be misconstrued by others as laziness. The same might be true of initiating things, the problem may simply be an inability to get started on a task, not a lack of desire.

Perhaps I could use an analogy here. An electricity-generating substation is geared to supply a certain number of volts to a given number of houses. If all those houses suddenly add several new appliances to the load and all switch on at the same time, the inability of the generator to supply the added voltage would be shown by a dimming of the lights. But the same effect might also be produced if a normal load was drawn and the wiring was damaged. My experience of brain injury is a bit like this. The 'dimming of the lights' in my case results in fatigue and a loss of strength. For someone like me who used to enjoy a good, long walk over the moors, a 15 minute walk into town becomes a route march. In fact when I left Rosehill, although I could walk reasonably well, I had to start using a wheelchair whenever I went out anywhere. Even when someone who used to enjoy engaging in certain sports or just playing ball with their children becomes a sufferer of brain injury, they become either completely unable to perform or simply run out of energy after just a few minutes' activity.

With Jordan, my son, at Torquay Marina, 1995.

This breakdown in the nervous system is, I feel, the reason why the many difficulties in mental functioning discussed in Chapter 3 arise, particularly the cognitive ones. Because the brain is working harder either to think things out or to react to the body's needs, it gets tired quicker and therefore decision-making and understanding takes longer, further tiring the brain. Writing this book is a classic example – it has taken much longer than it would have had I not had the injury, because I am unable to keep up the mental activity required for long periods of time. So I have to work for just an hour or two at a time rather than the several hours that an author usually would. That means that this chapter has taken almost three weeks to write in rough.

Adjusting to the reactions of family and friends

This subject may seem to be a strange one to include in long-term problems yet it needs to be remembered and understood that particularly when the sufferer returns to their home and social environment, often as far as they are concerned nothing has changed. Because of the damage their brain has sustained, some of their memories of who and what they were before – emotionally, mentally and in some cases physically – have been lost.

However, their family and friends do remember: it might be a glance, a look or smile, a way of walking or a personality trait that reminds them that a father, husband or friend has been taken away and replaced with a stranger who has many of the same characteristics. Some sufferers like myself do still have a sense of identity, with certain memories and an awareness of what has happened, but like their family and friends, they too have to make adjustments. One of the biggest is perceiving and understanding the perceptions and reactions of family and friends to the sufferer. Unbeknown to them, they may have changed in the way they walk, talk or act and therefore, either consciously or unconsciously, the family and friends react accordingly. If, like me, the sufferer remembers or thinks they remember how they were treated by certain people and then they detect a change or perceived change in the relationship, then they will react or overreact to that accordingly. Especially in the early stages of my brain injury I felt, rightly or wrongly I do not know, that some people thought I was slow or no longer bright. If I suspected this I would often react by ceasing the conversation or switching my attention to someone or something else.

The situation is a very difficult one for both sides, especially in the early days because as yet neither of them is aware that this will probably never change much, if ever. Some adjustments may need to come from the sufferer as they learn to adapt but more change will probably have to come from the family and friends. The old adage of 'give and take' will really have to come into play and it may be there will have to be more give on the part of the family and friends than of the sufferer. The speed and degree at which the relationship improves or deteriorates will in part be governed by mutual love, friendship, desire and commitment. Clearly for sufferers, families and friends there will be many long-term problems but they are not insurmountable. In the next chapter we will see some of the ways that sufferers can help themselves and later how the carers can help.

Chapter 8

Sufferers Can Help Themselves

Some may think that in the case of something as serious as brain injury, there is not much that sufferers can do to help themselves. However, nothing could be further from the truth. Beginning in the early days and going right on through life, with the correct knowledge, motivation and encouragement there are many avenues available which they can superintend themselves or follow under the guidance of carers.

Other treatment options

Most people would probably assume that healthcare ends at hospital and rehabilitation but in fact there are several alternative forms of treatment available. Whilst opinions on alternative medicine are a personal matter and vary greatly, some people in this 'enlightened' era still view alternative medicine as the next-best thing to witchcraft or as only used by 'New Age' people and the like.

However, many General Practitioners (GP – the British name for a medical doctor) up and down the country now have great confidence in and often refer difficult or unusual ailments to alternative healthcare practitioners. I have no desire here to raise any false expectations for anyone, so all I have done is outline just some of the forms of alternative healthcare available and give my own personal experiences with them.

Homoeopathy

This is something that Pauline and I had been using for several years before my accident. It had begun at first somewhat accidentally and we had gained so much confidence in it that for certain common ailments, e.g. bruises, colds and sore throats, it was nearly always our first line of defence. Pauline tells me that since I had a great amount of bruising on my face due to the fall, she found that one of the best treatments which helped me was arnica, as it helps either to reduce bruising or bring out subdued bruising. This was something we had used many times before with great success, especially with the children. However, an initial diagnosis and treatment for any complaint is best provided by a homoeopathic practitioner and will incur some expense.

Aromatherapy

I have no recollection of the use of this prior to my accident but I vividly remember it being used once I recovered from the coma. On several occasions a friend of ours who was a practitioner travelled down to Plymouth to apply some medication. I remember her massaging certain, what are called, essential oils into my feet and on several occasions I fell asleep and later had to apologize. However, she said that by doing so I had paid her a compliment because it showed I was completely relaxed which was the whole point of the exercise.

Thereafter both in hospital and at home for almost four years after the accident, Pauline used to have me breathe lavender oil whenever I was suffering a seizure or the auras prior to one. Lavender and/or eucalyptus oil helps to soothe the nerves and lower the level of anxiety.

For the brain itself and the symptoms following my injury, our friend used and showed Pauline how to use basil for activating the brain, bergamot to lift the spirits when feeling down and lavender for balancing the body and brain levels. What was also interesting was that just rubbing neat oils into the skin was no good, they had to be mixed with what was called a carrier oil such as olive oil to be effective.

It was several years before I found out how it worked. According to homeopaths, the molecules of each essential oil are a different shape. At the base of our nose we have two olfactory glands with little hairs inside. The oil molecules fit into the hairs according to the shape of the hairs and then send messages to the part of the brain which creates the seizure or anxiety or controls the part one is trying to reach. My friend who is an aromatherapist warns against the use of rosemary oil for those with brain damage. Thus I would always recommend seeking the advice of a trained practitioner before you try any aromatherapy or homeopathic remedies.

Muscle testing

This forms part of several types of alternative treatments. We had friends who used muscle testing and for several years they helped me make significant improvements in health. I will first of all briefly and in simple terms explain what muscle testing is and how it works.

The first principle of muscle testing is that each person's body knows what physical or psychological blocks are preventing it from healing and also knows what it needs to heal. In order to get this information from the body, the deltoid muscle in the upper arm is used. As the patient is asked a question, gentle pressure is applied to the outstretched arm – a positive answer will have no effect but a negative one will cause the arm to drop.

Through this method a skilled practitioner can determine the things that are causing the patient stress and the adjustments that need to be made – it could be that more rest, sleep, relaxation, a change of diet or even a combination of these things is needed. The body's energy lines or meridians can be used to make these adjustments – it is a similar principle to acupuncture and acupressure (but without the needles), a principle long known about and used, e.g. an ice cube held at the base of the thumb can help relieve toothache.

Armed with this knowledge, the practitioner works on the meridians which control the part of the body or brain which requires attention and then uses a variety of techniques including massage and certain homoeo-pathic remedies to bring relief and healing. As with all forms of medicine, be they formal or alternative, nothing is foolproof.

Naturopathic remedies

Sadly this word seems to conjure up in the minds of many people pictures of little old ladies drinking herbal teas. Teas made from the leaves, flowers, seeds and roots of various wild and garden trees and plants have been well known for centuries. Only in recent times has their efficacy for treating ailments, illnesses and body and brain damage been better understood and become more commonly used.

For years such herbs as valerian and skullcap have been used in reducing levels of tension and stress, and thus aiding restful sleep. They can be bought from your local health food shop as teas and liquids and are relaxants. It is therefore easy to see why such drinks and remedies are useful in helping those with brain injury but, as with most forms of alternative medicine, it would be wise to consult your GP for advice first or seek a consultation with a skilled practitioner in naturopathy.

Physiotherapy

The dictionary definition of physiotherapy is the treatment of disease by various physical agencies, e.g. exercise or heat, but not by drugs. Right from the outset in hospital and then on transfer to a rehabilitation unit, sufferers are included in a regime of physiotherapy. There may be a variety of reasons for this: a paralysis of some part of the body, a breakdown in hand–eye coordination or a deterioration of body muscle tone. So a series of exercises have been developed to work on these things but, as we shall see, they can be carried on at home without any special equipment or medical supervision.

Hand–eye coordination is often an early problem and, before the sufferer returns home, physiotherapists deal with this by something as simple as throwing and catching a ball. As can be seen, there is no special equipment or skills needed on the part of the carer except patience, kindness and persistence. There is one other benefit of this activity too: the sufferer can be helped to reintegrate with the family, especially the children, and I shall be returning to this later in the chapter.

Paralysis of one side or other of the body is quite common and can cause difficulties with hand, arm and/or leg movements, perhaps stiffness or spasticity. Exercises need to be geared towards encouraging movement, which really is a case of the brain relearning that it is possible and allowable to move certain body parts.

Since I was experiencing stiffness down my left side, I had, as I have mentioned before, my 'handbag hand'; that is, I tended to hold it at elbow level across my chest or stomach. To help me to change that, I needed to learn to relax my muscles and that it was alright to let my hand hang down. This was achieved by using play dough or plasticine. I would sit at a table for hours and roll the plasticine into a ball or sausage shape with the palm of my hand. I remember it being tiring and at times very frustrating. However, it did encourage a flexing of the fingers and muscles in my wrist and arm, helping them to relax. I also had to be reminded when walking to let my arm hang down by my side.

Relaxing the leg muscles was helped at the rehabilitation unit by working at a bar rather like a ballet dancer but without the tutu! We would hold onto the bar with one hand and bend and flex the knees. Doing this (also taking short walks and doing step-ups and downs) helped to loosen the muscles. Again, all these things can be done at home by the sufferer on their own or under supervision of the carer.

The loss of muscle tone, causing some flabbiness and/or stiffness, is worse if like me the sufferer had been involved in a physical job or a keep-fit regime. The way I was helped to regain muscle tone was by lifting weights, swimming, step-ups and downs, press-ups and walking. Apart from swimming and maybe lifting weights, all these things can be performed at home. As can be seen physiotherapy is yet another way that sufferers can help themselves or be helped on the road back to recovery.

Diet, exercise and activity

'Couch potato' is an expression most people are familiar with today and the usual TV portrayal is of someone who sits in front of the television all day, snacking on fattening foods and drinks (especially alcoholic drinks). But you might ask, what has this to do with recovering from brain injury? Simply, that a sufferer could easily follow or unintentionally be allowed by carers to follow the path to becoming a couch potato because of misplaced kindness or a misunderstanding of the sufferer's need for diet, exercise and activity. Because their ability to get around is perhaps limited and their mental abilities are jumbled up, it is very easy for the view to develop that the sufferer is unable to exercise and perform activities or that there is no longer any need for them to take care of their physical appearance.

Yet nothing could be further from the truth for two main reasons: first, the body of a brain injured person will deteriorate and suffer from a lack of these things just as much as that of an uninjured person and second, a lack of these things will stunt and retard any possible mental improvements and sense of purpose in life.

Diet

Considering that, especially in the early days when all involved are coming to terms with the changed situation, the sufferer may be inclined to spend much of their time resting, sleeping and doing nothing physical, it can readily be seen that there is a need to fairly quickly begin a regime of healthy eating and activity to stimulate the physical and mental processes – to start the sufferer on the road to some kind of recovery.

Even if they are physically restricted in some way, a diet will need to be arranged which takes into account their lack of movement. In other words, not too many fatty, starchy foods but plenty of fresh fruit, vegetables and fish. Not without good reason is fish called brain food and therefore what better food to be serving a sufferer? On this point, according to Christine Gorman in *Time* magazine, 30 October 2000, p.92, scientists in the USA say that certain fish, especially sardine, mackerel and salmon, contain nutrients called omega-3 fatty acids. Besides helping to regulate blood pressure, reducing the risk of blood clotting and heart disease, omega-3 provides the raw materials for, among other things, brain cells. Since our bodies cannot make their own omega-3, we need to get them from things we eat such as fish, flax, soybeans and walnuts.

Also when anyone, whether ill or in good health, spends a lot of time just lying or sitting around, there is an almost automatic tendency to want to eat. This is the tendency which needs to be curbed in sufferers unless it is for fresh fruit and water otherwise the weight will pile on, one's body condition will deteriorate as well as bring on the attendant problems of being overweight. The looks will also start to go!

A sufferer must never develop or be allowed to develop an attitude that it doesn't matter what they look like. Why allow an apparent lack of interest in themselves to emphasize a sufferer's condition? Besides, giving into that attitude will in time cause a lowering of their confidence and self-esteem, all of which can retard any improvement in the brain damage. So carers must beware thinking that they are being kind by not being too strict. The same can be said of exercise.

Exercise

As already stated in Chapter 3, one of the greatest problems a sufferer has to deal with is fatigue caused by a lack of stamina. Sufferers need to be taught to pace themselves so as not to overstretch their abilities. Just as the body and brain of a healthy person need a certain amount of rest to recover their strength and an unused muscle or limb can atrophy, so will a sufferer's body become lethargic and flabby without sufficient exercise.

When we talk about exercise we don't mean a workout at a gym or long distance running or swimming. Although none of these things must be considered impossible or improbable – as the old Chinese proverb goes, a journey of a thousand miles begins with a single step – so exercise must be gentle and regular at first. Your GP could suggest a mild regime of daily exercise but you could also devise your own.

A couple of widths (or lengths according to the person's ability) of swimming might be undertaken at least once a week. A daily walk around the block (or a walk of ten to 15 minutes) would be beneficial, as would a short jog once or twice a week, and/or a few minutes spent each day doing step-ups and downs on the bottom of a flight of stairs or several gentle press-ups on the floor.

Whether one breaks out in a sweat, becomes a little breathless or gets aches in the ankles or calves is not important. Nor does it matter whether the sufferer does all the above exercises or just one. What is important is that they do what they can manage comfortably, on a daily basis or, at the very least, weekly. The thing to remember is that exercising the body is exercising the brain too which can only be healthful. A healthy brain needs oxygen and what better way to do this than by exercise?

Activity

It has been said that a change in circumstances can literally change one's life – a chance to change careers, meet new friends or become involved in new activities. Brain injury certainly changes one's circumstances and life albeit unexpectedly. Whilst regular work may still be some way down the road and, because of certain psychological and physical problems, meeting new friends may seem too overwhelming, opportunities are perhaps now available to become involved in new activities.

Maybe the sufferer used to say that when they retired they would take up cross-stitch, writing, gardening, painting, learning to use a computer or maybe even take an Open University course to get a degree. As far as available time is concerned, to do these things or for other activities not yet considered the opportunity may never be better. The sufferer or the carer may feel that too many abilities have been lost to tackle any of these things. At the age of 44 I felt much the same way but as will be seen in the next chapter, I was very much mistaken.

Carers can do much to help sufferers take on new activities – by not setting the sufferer's sights too high so they become discouraged, by not allowing sedentary interests to cause the sufferer to avoid or postpone needed daily exercise and by encouraging any interest expressed by the sufferer or maybe even offer suggestions. Above all else, carers should be positive and enthusiastic and should commend for even small achievements. All of this can only have a positive effect on the sufferer's confidence and self-esteem. So what activities should be encouraged?

Dr Amir Soas of the Case Western Reserve University Medical School in Ohio is quoted by the *Vancouver Sun* newspaper (featured in the *Awake!* magazine, 22 May 2001) as saying to healthy people that the brain's vitality can remain intact throughout their lives as long as they keep exercising it. He says 'read, read, read'. To retain brain power as we age we are advised to 'choose mentally challenging hobbies, study a new language, learn to play a musical instrument or engage in stimulating conversation'. In other words 'anything that stimulates the brain to think'. He also encourages cutting back on television watching since at that time our brain 'goes into neutral'.

So if all of this is beneficial to healthy people, how much more so to those with brain injury? This therefore means that carers will need to be alert to the condition, improvement, abilities and needs of the sufferer and then choose or suggest activities that will stimulate the brain. Examples given in the Headway booklet *Activities for the Head Injured at Home* (Holford 1996) are that sufferers be given planning tasks such as a meal menu and preparation, also assigning daily and weekly tasks around the home and making choices regarding their dress. Not only will all of this stimulate them and prevent them becoming lethargic, it will also help them regain a feeling of self-worth. It will also help the carer practically, if only in a small way. Other ways that sufferers can be stimulated mentally is in finding pleasure in leisure activities.

Pleasure in leisure

This section is really, I suppose, a continuation of the previous one on activity but from a different angle. The old adage 'all work and no play makes Jack a dull boy' comes to mind here. It has long been acknowledged that a certain amount of leisure or recreation is needed for a healthy, balanced life for anyone of any age or condition. It would be very easy for sufferers and carers alike to see certain, what might otherwise be normally classed as leisure, activities only for their therapeutic value but with no pleasure.

To illustrate, suppose one's favourite occupation was reading the classics. However, if you were told that you had to read a certain amount of a certain piece by a certain date, what pleasure would there be in that? Or if you used to enjoy walking but were now told you had to walk a certain distance every so many days, again where would the pleasure be? So sufferers and carers need to realize that certain activities, whilst having a therapeutic benefit, should still be pleasurable and therefore should be pursued for their leisure potential and not always just for their therapeutic benefits. So walk, read or throw a ball just for the fun of it, not purely just because it will help with stamina or hand–eye coordination.

I don't know if it was intentional or not, but Rosehill worked on that principle. We had sessions every week where several clients would play group games such as Jenga. Although we knew we were doing this for certain therapeutic benefits, the games were made to be fun so we didn't see them as only work but also as leisure. Occasionally we would be taken out for a trip, either as a group in the minibus or as individuals in a car. Again, as with everything else, we were told of the benefits to ourselves but the trips were always made to be fun. So sufferers and carers need to learn, early on, not just to see activities from purely a therapeutic level but also as a form of pleasurable recreation, i.e. throwing a ball with the children not just as a means of helping reintegrate the sufferer with the family unit but as a form of fun.

Summary

I hope that it has been seen through the pages of this chapter that sufferers can do much to help themselves on the road back to recovery: they don't always have to have supervision or be in a hospital or rehabilitation unit environment. They could also look on their progress as having long- and short-term benefits, to themselves and to others. Looking back, I like to feel that this has been true of my recovery. Without wishing to sound arrogant, let me explain.

Chapter 9

Learning from the Experience of Brain Injury

A view held by many is that something good always comes from something bad. I personally don't subscribe to this view and since it also may not have been your experience in life so far, you may well be wondering, 'How can you say that you have learnt anything from your brain injury?'

From my own experience over the past seven or eight years, I can say that whilst it would not have been the way anyone would have chosen, I do feel that there have been benefits to me, other sufferers of brain injury, to Rosehill, to medical staff at Derriford and Torbay Hospitals, to carers of other sufferers, to professional bodies and even to victims of other ailments and their families. How? Let me elaborate.

To myself and other sufferers

The very fact that I have written this book is, I hope, just one positive outcome: if the accident had not happened then neither would the book. As I mentioned in the Preface, I was first encouraged to write this by one of the OTs at Rosehill, as a help to others but also as a therapy for myself. It is said by some that it can be therapeutic or cathartic to write about an experience one has had: to clarify it in one's mind, to make a record whilst it is still fresh or quite simply to get it out of one's system, especially if it was a particularly unpleasant experience.

I suppose, for me, just writing this has been useful in clarifying it in my mind and making a record of my thoughts and feelings and of the things that happened to me and my family whilst the memory is still fresh. Someone may ask why I would want to make such a record, surely I would want to just forget? My answer would be that if there is no record, how in the future will I be able to help others if I cannot recall the details?

Also since we had no books to guide us, we have had to learn much by trial and error over the past years. I wouldn't want anyone else to have to go through what we did without some form of help. So to others like me and their carers, this book will I hope prove to be a guide; giving them advice and encouragement but most of all, hope that there really is life after brain injury.

It seems from my experience, and that of others, that sufferers of brain injury initially run the gamut of feelings of worthlessness, hopelessness, helplessness and depression among others, and these feelings may continue either as an occasional or a permanent feature of their lives depending on the person, their condition and their mental attitude.

My condition has taught me many things about myself and others. For example, having lost several skills and abilities that I had taken for granted for years such as driving, working, singing, being the breadwinner and even having full hearing. I have learned how determined I can be in dealing with these losses, in coping with my disabilities and in achieving new skills (more on this in a moment).

Whilst the loss of these skills has naturally caused occasional bouts of depression and at times a feeling of grieving, I soon realized that dwelling on them was unproductive and could not bring them back. I found it not only more worthwhile to be positive and do something beneficial but it also made people want to be around me.

Looking back before the accident, hard as it is to admit, I had not been very tolerant and understanding of other people's problems whether they were health related, emotional or otherwise. Yet following the accident, since I expected and received help and understanding from others outside the medical field, I feel that I have in turn learned to be more sympathetic and empathetic towards others. Whereas before I did not express much patience with others, I now try harder to understand and make allowance for them because I expected and received it from others. I think this point was driven home to me recently when Pauline and I watched a documentary about Sir Harry Secombe[1] which followed his stroke, diagnosis of prostrate cancer and then his death. We watched his treatment, therapy and progress towards getting back to some sort of normal life.

What was interesting was that what kept him going was his faith, his sense of humour and the setting of goals and reaching them. This was the first time since my accident that I was able to watch and talk about someone in a similar condition to me without it reducing me to tears. Sir Harry said that coming home was the hardest thing, seeing his record of achievements on the wall (discs, photos etc.) and realizing he would never do most of them again. I fully understood exactly what he meant.

Perhaps I have also been helped in this by learning more about the brain. As I have already said, the lack of books on brain injury is partly what led me to write this one but there have been several excellent programmes on television regarding the brain, its functions, some of the things which can cause it to fail to function properly and more generally what medical science has learned in recent years about it.

Learning what I can has made me more receptive to information regarding other health problems. On this matter I have particularly found the *Awake!* magazine (a bi-monthly magazine published by Jehovah's Witnesses) to be very helpful as it deals with many real life experiences. This in turn has made me realize that I am not alone in my injury and experience and it helps me to remember that there are other people worse off than one's self.

Surprisingly my accident did something else for me that I wouldn't before have thought possible: it helped to strengthen my faith in and reliance on God. As Jehovah's Witnesses, my family and I already had a belief in God and I feel that I have seen His hand in my life straight after and following the accident. I can honestly say that I have spent more time in prayer since then than at any other time in my life.

Realizing at the beginning that working and driving were likely to be a long way down the road if not impossible meant that I needed, for my own self-confidence, to acquire other skills and I now had the time to do that. As Penny Weekes, one of the OTs, said to me before I was discharged from Rosehill for good, I had been given an opportunity that not many men of my age get: to change vocation or occupation midway through life.

So this led me towards writing but not before making several attempts to get back into employment. Though I didn't at the time appreciate that employment either full- or part-time was possibly beyond my capabilities, despite still being a day patient at Rosehill I began in January 1996 the first of several attempts to regain my lost role, i.e. my function as family breadwinner. When that appeared to fail (more on this in Chapter 11) I started trying to cast my net wider.

Following the suggestion made at Rosehill about trying writing and even whilst I was still there, I began writing a handbook on salesmanship. From these jerky, uncertain beginnings I eventually wrote and had published my first article. Then after I went on to write and have published ten other articles in Britain and Malta, I finally decided it was time to make a concerted effort to write this book for which I had been doing research and collecting material.

From my forays into writing came yet another benefit. Up until 1998, I had been typing up my material on an old Silver Reed typewriter which I had had for almost 20 years. When my doctor heard that I was writing seriously, he gave me a fairly new electric typewriter. My typing was a slow, two finger affair, so to try and speed it up I went to my local Adult Learning

Centre and took a Computer Literacy and Information Technology (CLAIT) typing course which increased my typing speed from eight words per minute (wpm) to 23 wpm in just six weeks.

With this start and because I could see the advantages to myself, I used some of the money I had received for my articles to buy a secondhand computer from a friend. Believe me, that was one of the best moves I made, especially after I acquired a printer. Although both our boys are 'computer literate' and helped me out when I got stuck, which I still do regularly, I more or less taught myself from a new computer magazine on sale at that time.

One final thing I was able to do, since I now had the time, was to begin to learn British Sign Language to enable me to converse with the large number of deaf friends we have and also to have a form of communication available to me in case my good right ear ever gives out and I become totally deaf. I must be honest, this was the first thing since my accident where I temporarily had to admit defeat as I found it to be beyond my capabilities. However, now that Pauline and Jordan have both taken and passed courses in British Sign Language, I feel I will try again later.

So these have been just a few of the unexpected consequences of my brain injury and I hope they will be of some help to others like me and their families. Whilst life will change after brain injury it need not necessarily be the end of quality life. There is still much one can do for life to be purposeful. I said in the beginning I felt there were benefits to others too so let us look at them.

To carers of other sufferers

I suppose that the positive aspects of my brain injury for carers of other sufferers was highlighted on the evening of 9 February 2000 when I gave a presentation to Rosehill Carers' Support Group entitled 'Brain Injury from the Patient's Perspective'. Apart from there being more in attendance than at any other meeting, so I was told, I felt the comments from the carers themselves made the meeting all the more worthwhile. After a one hour talk, there was a question and answer session for another quarter of an hour.

Several people made encouraging comments to me and one in particular came from a middle-aged couple with a brain injured son whose marriage had broken up because of his condition. They said that before that evening they had despaired for their son and them-selves, feeling that there was no hope and that nothing more could be done. They said that hearing my experi-ences had given them encouragement for a renewed hope and a purpose in life to work towards.

To victims of other conditions and their families

About 14 years ago a close family friend suffered a work-related head injury. Apart from breaking both wrists and having concussion, he didn't seem to have any serious after-effects and just went back to a reasonably normal life. Then two or three years ago, Pauline, James and I detected in him an indication of some of the same symptoms of brain injury that I had in my early days: he was slowing down in his thought processes and speech patterns. We were obviously concerned over this and made mention of it to his wife. She also expressed concern, saying that both she and their daughters had noticed he was slowing up, almost as in old age, yet like me he was only 50 years old. Since he was not aware of his condition he refused to get a medical opinion but when he lost the use of his left hand (he was a painter and decorator) he realized there was something seriously wrong.

He made an appointment to see his doctor who promptly referred him to a neurologist who diagnosed Parkinson's disease (not related to the accident). They were devastated, as were we, but at least they were comforted in finding that something could be done to help him which would have been impossible had it been brain injury. When he eventually came to terms with the fact of his condition, he said to his wife that he hoped he could be as positive and determined as I was.

113

To the rehabilitation unit

I feel that Rosehill and their techniques are greatly responsible for my current condition and state of health, and I hope also that I have in part repaid that debt by having made such a good recovery. Without wishing to sound at all presumptuous, I like to feel that my recovery is itself a benefit to Rosehill. Though I am not a rarity as a success story for them, I am sure they would be the first to admit that with the best will in the world and not because of any fault on their part, it is not always possible for them to achieve successful outcomes for clients. Of the 30 clients at Rosehill when I was there, at least three died then or since.

Yet of the others, one has gone on to travel the south west of England giving presentations on the Alexander technique and another returned to school in his previous profession as a teacher, teaching children to use computers. He also became a major organizer of a local operatic and dramatic society. And then there is me. So when it is the considered view of many people that brain injury means the end of quality life, then perhaps my brain injury has had some advantages for Rosehill when sufferers like myself contradict this preconception.

To professional bodies

Yet another positive consequence has been that I have been able to give presentations to certain professional bodies, some on behalf of Rosehill. Around September to October 1997 Bill Grove, formerly a client manager at Rosehill, was helping another rehabilitation group called Robinia to set up a unit near Taunton. To help raise awareness of brain injury, Robinia and their work and to show what a rehabilitation unit could achieve, I was asked to go up and give a presentation to an invited audience of managers and staff from social services, health authorities and the Headway organization from Somerset and Avon, Wiltshire and Devon. There was also a solicitor. On 30 October 1998 I gave a similar presentation to a group of solicitors involved with litigation cases on behalf of clients with head injuries. The purpose was to help them understand what they would be dealing with and therefore be able to make a better case for their clients when claiming damages.

I suppose the most nerve-racking experience was giving a presentation to an audience of neurology personnel and local Disability Employment Advisors (DEAs) at Torbay Hospital in Torquay, on 14 June 2000 (see photo overleaf). From the feedback received by Rosehill and myself, it seems true that my experience has helped many professional people directly or indirectly involved with brain injury, its treatment and its legal implications.

Giving a talk to neurosurgeons and DEAs at Torbay Hospital, June 2000.

To hospital staff

Without wishing to appear immodest, I like to feel that my time in both Derriford and Torbay Hospitals has been of some little help to the staff. Let me explain what I mean. A few days after I regained consciousness Paul Francel sat on the side of my bed and explained that I had brain injury. He told me that when I first went down for surgery I was in such a bad state that some on the neurology team more or less felt that because I was so badly smashed up, there was very little they could do for me. When I asked him why he had even tried he said he was 'a sucker for lost causes'.

116

I am sure that because of his skill and positive attitude and my determination to live, others of that team will have benefited. I also know that because of their work on me the physiotherapy teams at both hospitals were greatly encouraged on seeing me many months later. I left Derriford almost unable to walk but a few months later they were pleased to see me greatly improved.

Conditions such as epilepsy or traumatic brain injury have opened up new areas of research in medical science. Through understanding these and other deficits in brain functioning, medical scientists have been able to reach a fuller understanding of how the brain works and consequently use this knowledge to help those, such as myself, with brain injuries.

Some of the nurses were greatly surprised over the care and attention given me by my many friends from my religious faith. One nurse in particular at Derriford was, she said, helped by me. She was suffering marital problems at the time but she said she felt better for the advice I gave her on dealing with her situation, and my own positive attitude to marriage and life in general. I tell you all this not to make myself sound like an angel but just to show that one never knows how they can help other people, directly and indirectly.

Summary

I hope you will agree that there can be positive aspects of brain injury, albeit unexpected. But you may feel that all this is very introverted and selfish, sufferers thinking only of themselves. However, that is not the impression I want to give, carers and families are very much affected and need help. As I said early on, we had to learn much of our experience by trial and error, of which this book is the result. So now I want to spend some time looking at how carers can cope with caring for a sufferer, not forgetting themselves and their families.

Note

1.   Sir Harry Secombe was a popular British entertainer.

Chapter 10

Caring

How to Cope

Coming to terms with the diagnosis

Caring for a sufferer is a huge responsibility and the initial shock can be overwhelming. Although from my own experience this is not a common occurrence, the person who becomes the carer can go into denial after hearing of or seeing the condition of a sufferer. The carer may go into shock – they hear the news but feel numb, as though they are physically here but not mentally or emotionally and just function on autopilot. If the victim was struck down away from home or if they had not seen each other for some time, this condition of going into denial may be more likely to arise.

It has been described as being rather like the grieving over someone who has died. The ones left behind experience thoughts and feelings such as, 'It can't be true, I only saw them this morning' or 'There must be a mistake, I was talking to them on the phone yesterday.' I am sure that all of us can understand or identify with this especially if we have lost a loved one in death – we find it hard to accept or believe that the one who was with us only a few hours ago is not coming back, ever. Really what happens to the carer is rather the same as what happens to a sufferer – the shock causes the brain to be unable or unwilling to accept the loss. It also causes some of the same emotions – anger, frustration and resentment.

Whether the injury is work-related, driving-related or the result of an attack, anger may be directed at the victim for not taking more care or even against the carer themselves, 'I shouldn't have let them go out today.' Frustration may come from several things: 'I wish I could turn the clock back', 'What if I hadn't let them go out today?' and 'I've always told them to be more careful doing that or going there.' The resentment may simply be, 'Why did it have to happen to them? They were the salt of the earth, wouldn't do a wrong thing to anyone yet there are lots of rogues around who just seem to get by without anything happening to them, why didn't it happen to them?' Any one or all of these feelings could occur, especially if the carer and the victim had not spoken before parting or had had a difference of opinion so that the last words they had together were unkind. Then the carer feels another emotion, guilt.

It can therefore be seen that denial can take many forms, some functional, others dysfunctional. Not accepting the permanence or extent of the disability could be favourable if a positive outlook encouraged rehabilitation but could have the opposite effect if unrealistic expectations mean that failure is inevitable.

So how can carers come to terms with the diagnosis? By accepting the fact that accidents do happen, even to our loved ones, and that the only way to avoid this is for one to be tied to a chair in a room in a house and that just isn't realistic. I raise all these points, not to make anyone feel worse than they maybe already do, but to help them see that they are not unique in having these feelings but that they are quite natural.

Learning to deal with sufferers' feelings

I have already covered, in Chapter 4, some of the feelings the sufferer experiences. I would like now to look at frustration from a different angle; also embarrassment and guilt. Carers may assume especially in the early days that sufferers have none of these feelings at all but are only concerned with themselves and their own situation. That may be true of some but not all.

If the carer can understand how the sufferer is feeling and why, it may help them both to deal better with their situation. This is not as difficult as it may at first seem. I hope to show this by my personal experiences but carers will learn much from their own experience as time goes by and also by remembering that if they deal negatively with the sufferer then the results will be negative.

The key really is having empathy – the ability to put one's self in the shoes of another person. For example, try to imagine having had the ability to programme a video recorder and then losing that ability and having to be told by someone, especially a stranger, how to work the video, even how to rewind or fastforward to find a certain programme. Just imagine the frustration, anger and even the embarrassment of such a situation for a sufferer. I know, I have been there. If the carer can sympathize with this scenario then there will be less tension between them and the carer will be on the way to understanding how the sufferer is feeling.

I am sure many people can remember having made a social gaffe – the occasion when, either with an individual or group of friends or strangers, you said or did something which caused a deathly hush to descend. Then you wished the floor would open up and swallow you. The embarrassment that causes is almost painful and worse so if our families are present. If the carer can identify with this situation then they will find it easier to understand the way the sufferer is feeling just then.

Yes, some sufferers do feel a deep sense of embarrassment when they commit such a social blunder before others, whether friends or strangers, or when they display a difficulty with or lack of understanding for an apparently simple thing. Maybe they have an occasional emotional outburst or an unacceptable form of social behaviour with someone of the opposite sex or they just do something that they know they wouldn't have done before the injury. They probably feel guilty about embarrassing their families.

If the carer realizes that the sufferer is already feeling bad about the situation, then chastising them like a naughty child or retaliating with a sharp word will not solve the situation but will likely only add to the tension. What will also help is remembering that nine times out of ten, the sufferers can't help themselves and probably don't mean to do whatever it is they do.

Frustration may also result because some sufferers have difficulty expressing themselves. Carers should therefore try to resist the inclination to butt in and guess the word the sufferer is hunting for. Rather they should give them time to think, whilst perhaps suggesting a word or two but not too many as this may frustrate or anger them. They can also tell them that it will probably come back when they are not thinking about it, then change the subject.

The frustration may come from a memory loss or an inability to perform simple tasks. Carers can help by perhaps giving a verbal reminder or even writing it down. The one thing they must remember whenever presenting information to a sufferer is to always give it in small amounts as too much information at one time can overload the system and create more anger and frustration.

Sufferers may also become frustrated when they know what they want to say but the brain and/or tongue can't get it out fast enough to be able to take part in a conversation. Carers must be sure to still include the sufferer in conversations but not to change the subject too often as this can give them too much to cope with. Still on the thought of conversation, carers must be sure to include sufferers in family discussions if possible or else they may feel isolated and ignored and then their frustration will increase. And never use expressions like 'I'll be back in two seconds' because the sufferer may take it literally and that is exactly what they will expect and when the carer isn't, the sufferer may get distraught, frustrated or angry.

One final point, further patience will be required by carers when they hear the sufferer repeat the same story over and over again. This is a condition known as perseveration and is also common in older people and those with Alzheimer's. And also when the sufferer gives the impression that they are the only ones who are important, as this makes them at times very demanding.

So summarizing, carers may feel that this is an awful lot to accomplish and that they are having to give in a lot to the sufferer. But please take it from me that living with brain injury is not going to be easy to begin with and there is no quick fix. However, if carers try to apply some of these suggestions, it will make life easier for all concerned. This will be accomplished if carers learn to understand how the sufferer is feeling, which they will be able to do if they can exercise empathy, sympathy, patience and love.

All of this might be covered by applying the Golden Rule, 'Do unto others as you would have them do unto you.' If carers can be understanding towards sufferers, they may be able to help them get back to some sort of average[1] life more quickly. Much of what we have said here might also be applied to the other changes in the sufferer, the psychological ones.

Handling the psychological changes

The carer may only remember the sufferer before the injury as having been a kind, pleasant, gentle, even-tempered individual. Now this person perhaps has outbursts of anger, impatience and irritability among other things and is generally very hard to live with. Though it may seem strange, the brain injured person despite their injury and even their conduct may care deeply about the carer even though they don't show it or express it.

Carers could ask themselves, if they and the sufferer had known about what was going to happen, what would he/she have wanted for them now?

Well, the carer has various options of how to handle these changes: by realizing and accepting that things have changed and may or may not ever improve, by trying to be understanding or by retaliating to or ignoring the sufferer's psychological changes. In this changed situation and environment, I am sure that most people would want to remember the good times and would constantly compare how the sufferer is now to how they were before. That is only to be expected but in the long-term it is counterproductive, things have changed and will never improve without thinking positively, perhaps asking themselves what they can do to help minimize the anger, impatience and irritability.

Maybe they know that a certain course of action by themselves or the sufferer produces one of these conditions, so they can perhaps head it off before it arises. It could be that going to a certain place, watching a certain film or programme, performing a certain task or even just meeting certain people brings back unhappy memories for the sufferer and the reactions that follow. If so then the carer could change the arrangements. This may seem logical but it highlights the need for the carer to be constantly on the watch regarding the sufferer's life pattern and experiences and reactions to these.

Things may not change immediately but life will become easier for both if they are constantly aware of what stresses the sufferer and efforts are made to avoid it. The rehabilitation unit should also be able to offer advice to the carer on this.

If the carer retaliates in kind whenever the sufferer has a verbal outburst, it will probably solve nothing but instead aggravate the situation. If the sufferer is chastised and treated like a child, then the result may well be what would be expected from a child. If the sufferer is an adult, even though they act like a child, they may well resent being treated like one. So when, for example, the sufferer is being irrational, difficult or argumentative, rather than just being drawn in, stop and consider, 'Why are they acting this way? What's causing this? Are there too many people talking at once or is there too much background noise?'

If the carer remembers what has happened to the brain of the sufferer, as discussed in Chapter 3, maybe they will be better able to deal with the situation rather than just retaliate verbally. Whilst taking on the role of a therapist would be impossible, wrong and inappropriate, having extra understanding could help them steer a smoother path through the difficult times and as a consequence help all concerned.

As can be seen, being a carer of someone who has experienced psychological changes due to a brain injury is somewhat of a minefield. And getting through a real minefield safely is only possible by either physically following a person who knows the way or by following their written instructions. Whilst these suggestions on handling the psychological changes do not purport to be the only or all the suggestions available, they are a record of what I have seen my family apply to my condition and what I am aware of having done to myself and others.

It might seem that carers have a lot to do in dealing with the changes and it is true, they do. Especially in the early days, carers should not generally expect much of those with brain injury, there will be a lot of 'give and take' with the carer doing much of the giving. A lot will be based on their own observations since every sufferer is different and what is written here is simply a guide.

Avoiding overprotection but being safe

When someone suffers a brain injury, one of the first things that is stressed to the carers, especially when the sufferer is returning home, is the need for them to protect their head. The carers are warned that a blow to the head or even just a slight knock could produce a blood clot or at worst be fatal. Therefore it can be seen how carers can become overprotective even to the point of paranoia.

The first step towards avoiding that situation, but still keeping the sufferer safe, is to be realistic. Really any person whether young or old, well or ill may at any time suffer a blow to the head which could produce a blood clot, e.g. a child may fall over when playing, an adult may walk into a door or a driver may bang their head if they brake suddenly. Something else which may help keep things in their proper perspective is to try and see things as a parent (even if the carer isn't).

When a child goes to school for the first time, their parent doesn't want to leave them. Then when they start coming home with cuts and bruises or the other kids are going down with head lice, whooping cough or some other childhood complaint, the parent wants to keep their child home to protect them. Then perhaps if the child goes up to secondary or grammar school and begins to be bullied, the parent wants to sort it out for them. At the time they just think they are being protective but probably years later they realize they were being *overprotective.*

The same could be true of carers. They must remember that they can't wrap the sufferer up in cotton wool – they have to be allowed to get on with life, otherwise life will never be 'normal' or have any quality to it. So the next thing that carers have to do, to avoid overprotection but keep the sufferer safe, is to take all the practical, sensible and reasonable precautions they can.

Rosehill told Pauline of the advisability of putting warning signs on high cupboard doors. This was to remind me that if I opened the doors, I must remember to close it before I bent down to avoid the risk of forgetting it was open and then coming up fast. This proved to be a very wise precaution and even after seven years, although the signs are no longer there, I am still very aware when I open high cupboard doors. However, despite this safety measure in the early days, I still seemed to be quite accident-prone and banged my head occasionally in any number of places. Finally it was suggested I wore protective head gear in the form of a bicycle helmet, to limit the risk, even when I went out.

Wearing bicycle helmet to protect head.

One other area where carers could be overanxious is in trying to be overprotective of a sufferer who would like to take up driving. No one must assume that because someone has suffered brain injury, they will never drive again. Depending on the individual and their injury, given time and retraining they may be able to once again obtain a licence, provided they have not had an epileptic seizure in less than one year. If carers are concerned about a sufferer driving again, I suggest they read the Headway leaflet, 'Driving after a Head Injury'.

So if the carer is realistic and sensible, they can remove much of the worry and fear from their lives and the sufferer can feel unfettered, protected and safe.

Looking after oneself – Help for the carer

If anyone has ever watched a nature programme about how animals and birds care for their young, they will probably have seen how intensive the care is around the clock and wondered how the parent manages to keep going. Human parents will recognize the analogy when they remember caring for their newly born infant. Parents are constantly on the go: feeding, cleaning, dressing, changing nappies and caring for the child's every need. Really, the same is true of carers with sufferers.

The condition of the sufferer and the extent to which they need help will determine the amount of work that a carer has to do and the reserves they will have to draw on physically, emotionally and mentally. I think it will be true to say that with all sufferers, the first few weeks at home will be the hardest for the carers. Only then will they find out what the needs are of their sufferer and what caring for them involves. So carers will need to pace themselves and keep themselves fit and well if they are to carry the main weight of responsibility for the next 10, 20 or 40 years. How are they going to cope with preserving their own physical, emotional and mental health for the long haul?

This is also the time when the carer has to acknowledge several things: there are only so many hours in a day and they only have a certain amount of reserves to draw on. If they are part of a family, they could call on other members to help out and not be afraid to delegate. If friends offer to help, carers should not feel that it is all their responsibility or that friends are imposing. They should consider all offers gladly and willingly, provided the friends know what is involved and the carer feels safe leaving the sufferer in their care.

Carers not only need help to cope with the workload but they also need rest, relaxation and time to themselves. It is easy to see how they can become so absorbed in caring for the sufferer's needs, they forget that they have needs too, especially if they are caring for a family as well. Therefore carers must make sure that they get enough rest and sleep, if possible putting off making any major decisions until they feel less stressed and can fully concentrate. Something else they might do if necessary is ask their GP for a sick note.

If possible, they should also share worries and problems – talking to other people can often help prevent stress from building up. Talk to family, friends, professionals or maybe even someone you feel you can confide in at your place of worship. The important thing is to talk to someone they trust and have confidence in. As will be discussed in Chapter 11, there are many organizations they can turn to for help, even a solicitor who specializes in personal injury litigation if necessary. Besides all of these, carers must make sure that they regularly have a break whether that just be a few hours, a night out, a weekend or even a week away from the pressures of caring.

This might be done by calling upon the help of family or friends (one should be judicious because not everyone can or knows how to cope) or, alternatively, there is a special arrangement available for carers called respite care. This is where qualified carers take over the care of the sufferer either at home or in an institution. This can usually be arranged through a local carers' group, social services, a family GP or the rehabilitation unit which originally cared for them.

Something else the carer would be wise to remember is that when making decisions and dealing with professional people, be sure to take the whole family into consideration, not just the sufferer. The carer and sufferer should both be involved in goal setting as Pauline and I both were at Rosehill. And carers should never feel shy of asking questions about things they don't understand.

Carers also must never feel selfish in thinking of their own needs or guilty about having fun. They must not give up any hobbies, interests or outings: they will need them now more than ever. They should probably bear in mind that if they 'crack up', they will be of no use to themselves or the sufferer. There may also be the needs of others to take care of, for example children.

The needs of children

It can be seen that the sufferer can easily absorb so much of the time and energy of the carer that if there are children in the family, they can unintentionally be neglected. There is a danger that the carer will give most of their time and attention to the sufferer, unfortunately forgetting that the children need them as well even if they are older.

Sadly, there are several dangers inherent in this situation. Children may feel rejected by the carer, especially if they had been close before the brain injury. Also, even if they had been close to the sufferer before the injury, the child may now be resentful of them because of all the time and energy being spent on them to the apparent exclusion of the child and perhaps because the sufferer can no longer spend time with them, playing games or engaging in a mutual interest or hobby. A child may feel anger towards the brain injured parent as my youngest son Jordan did. The child may be angry at the sufferer because they were not more careful so as to avoid the injury. All of these are very real, important and explosive as far as the child is concerned and more so if the child is young since they don't yet have the knowledge and experience to understand their feelings. So it is clear that the needs of the children are as important as (although different to) those of the sufferer.

Just as carers must do for themselves, they must be sure to make time for their children. This can be done in small and large ways, like remembering to take the child in their arms or just to smile. Even if they feel worn out, this will reassure the child that they are loved and cared for. Especially if the child is small one must try not to push them away when they seek attention. Carers and sufferers need to show interest in and spend time with their children to try and combat any feelings of rejection children may already feel.

Although these things should be practised on a daily basis, something parents can do, once the sufferer is home and life settles into some sort of routine, is set a specific time aside each week to do something or to go somewhere with the children because they need a break away from the home occasionally too – a schedule may well help in making sure this happens. Being aware of children's needs and, if appropriate, involving them in caring will help parents when children appear to be experiencing difficulties – parents may be better able to detect the reasons why and deal with them and head them off before they get out of hand. Therefore this will help avoid much unnecessary grief and instead help maintain unity and cohesion in the family unit so all will benefit. This then is just one hope, among others, that the family touched by brain injury can keep in mind – but there are disappointments also.

Hopes and disappointments

Logically and naturally, there will be many hopes entertained by the carer of a brain injured person and there will possibly be disappointments that are not expected. Most carers will come to know and accept that the sufferer will never be exactly as they were before their injury. The best they can hope for is that they may regain some of their lost skills and abilities and that life may take on some form of 'normality'.

They may read my account of living with brain injury and hope that this will happen to the one they care for. I would wish the same for them but, being realistic, the chances are slim, especially when I consider the number of clients originally at Rosehill compared with the number who left to go back to some form of 'normal' life. However, if carers keep a diary of the sufferer's progress, it may be useful to look back on and help them realize that progress has been made.

So the disappointments may range from the sufferer not returning home or not regaining certain physical or mental abilities, through to not being able to partake in a normal family and social life. But one of the biggest disappointments for the carer, if the sufferer is a partner, is the possible breakdown of the marriage. This is not being negative but is based partly on studies carried out on such families and also on the fact that of the four of us who left Rosehill at the same time to return to a 'normal' life, the marriages of two suffered breakdown. Though I have no figures to back up these points, I informed that it is quite a common occurrence. This not to say that the carers did not love their partners or that they didn't try hard to come to terms with their situation but for some people there is just too much to cope with.

On hearing several years ago of the break-up of the marriage of one of my companions at Rosehill, I said to Pauline that besides feeling sad at the news I couldn't understand the carer leaving the sufferer at such a critical time in their life, of how thoughtless and unloving they must have been. She then explained to me some of the emotional, mental, physical and financial pressures of caring that may contribute to a carer not wanting a sufferer home. She said that any one of these pressures plus sex-related problems could be the cause of the breakdown. In fact she said that at times she had felt pushed to the limit and that the main things that had kept us together was the fact that she loved me and took our faith and marriage vows seriously.

So the carer must be prepared for the possibility of this greatest disappointment of all, even after striving to care for their marriage partner. But the fact that two out of the four of us who left Rosehill together have maintained their marriages shows that a carer must not view a marriage break-up as inevitable. They must work hard as they did before the injury – at least, however, forewarned is forearmed as they say.

Summary

As already mentioned, carers must never feel that they have to suffer in silence when caring for a brain injured person. There are several organizations available which can be contacted and would be only too pleased to help and offer advice if they can. In the next chapter, I have endeavoured to explain the function of some of these and how they might help.

On holiday, Majorca 2001.

Note

1. I use the word 'average' where 'normal' would have seemed to be the correct word. This is because medical personnel used to stress to me that brain injured people are not abnormal!

Chapter 11

Useful Information and Sources

Much of this information may only be applicable to those living in the United Kingdom because of the National Health Service (NHS) and certain brain injury organizations. However, some countries may have similar systems and organizations, so carers and sufferers will need to make use of whatever bodies are available. I have also included additional information about such things as applying for a job and this may I hope prove useful elsewhere than in just the UK.

Social services

It may be recalled that in Chapter 5, I explained how representatives of social services were present at my initial interview at Rosehill in order to determine my condition and needs. My recollection is that they really came into their own when I returned home. Because my balance was still very bad in the early days, I had great difficulty in standing up under the shower and walking safely up stairs. Hence I was first provided with a plastic bath seat which lay across the bath and enabled me to take a shower sitting down.

To increase my safety on steps and stairs, I was provided with a new handrail for the stairs inside the house and handrails for the steps at the front and rear of the house outside. All of these things were provided swiftly and free of charge so I can only praise social services for their help in making my life safer and giving my family peace of mind.

Department of Social Security (DSS)

I know that the DSS in Britain has received much criticism at times and I have been guilty of my share because of the size, amount and regularity of forms that occasionally have to be filled in and sometimes because of the slowness in receiving payments. However, I must say this in their defence: since my income was terminated abruptly the day I fell and we had no other source of income, the DSS stepped into the breach and as a family we have not since then had a week go by when we have not received a payment to take care of our material needs.

Some may say, 'Well you only received what you were due for paying in National Insurance stamps for all your working life.' This is very true but I have to say that we have not, by and large, had to fight for our money and even now, seven or eight years down the road, we are still receiving enough to survive – 'just'. True, we cannot often buy what we used to class as luxuries but we manage – in fact I am now allowed to work part-time and earn therapeutic earnings, a little extra which helps (more on that later). On a more light-hearted note – back to the thought of not having to fight for our money – in one particular year not long after my return home, due they tell me to a clerical error, we several times received double the weekly amount of money we were due (which we of course returned promptly).

One of the biggest problems, which I feel arises for carers in families where the breadwinner is struck down in some way, is knowing just what government benefits they are eligible to claim for and how to claim. If I do have a complaint to make against the DSS it is that although the information is out there, in our experience we found that the onus was on us to know about and look for it. Of course, until someone is in that situation they don't know what they need. And in our opinion, the forms are not really geared towards head injury but more towards physical disability.

Carers in this situation fortunately have available to them four avenues of help: the rehabilitation unit, Citizens' Advice Bureau (CAB), local or national carers' associations (more on that in a moment) and people they know who might have been in a similar situation. If the sufferer has gone straight away to a rehabilitation unit, then the unit will very quickly provide the carer with the necessary information.

However, before they can claim for anything they will need a sick note for the sufferer (and they may even be able to get one for themselves eventually) which will mean a visit to the GP who may, depending on the condition of the sufferer, supply a permanent sick note. This will enable the carer to apply for, among other things, income support benefit and/or incapacity benefit. Another benefit available may be housing, which would mean they may get help with their rent or mortgage and council tax. Receiving any or all of these benefits would be a great relief to the family and relieve them of many of the financial worries if the sufferer was the main source of income.

There may be other benefits available but since information about benefit entitlement is not always forthcoming, it will be up to the carer to do research. One tip I would like to share is to suggest that family members check any life insurance or mortgage endowment policies in force. Do not take it for granted that if the sufferer had no accident insurance, they therefore had no accident cover. We had a pleasant surprise from our mortgage endowment policy which unknown to us stated that if I suffered an injury meaning I could not work, then the insurance company took over the payment of our monthly premiums as normal until such time as either I could work again or the policy matured. So do check.

One more piece of advice: when filling out benefit claim forms, whether new or renewals, carers or family members should read them very carefully and not fill them in if they are unsure of anything. In fact in the early days, I would recommend that they seek the help of the rehabilitation unit, GP and/or CAB. It is a very strange thing but benefit forms are so phrased and laid out that using the wrong terminology to describe a condition or event can mean the difference between receiving a benefit or not.

I am not suggesting in any way that the DSS deliberately set out to catch people out but I accept that because of the great amount of benefit fraud committed, they are constantly having to be on guard against fraudsters. So carers should seek expert help before they launch themselves at any form with a pen. Since the forms often have to be renewed annually, carers will regularly receive new ones, so will probably become quite adept at filling them in. However, since the forms keep changing, if carers and family members are unsure of anything, it might still be advisable to seek expert help.

Headway – the brain injury association

To explain who or what Headway is, I can do no better than give a summary of a letter sent to me by them following a request for information.

They are the leading UK charity dedicated to the care and support of people with head injury and were set up in 1979 to respond to the needs of a growing number of people surviving a head injury. The organization exists to 'promote understanding of all aspects of head injury and to provide information, support and services to people with head injury, their families and carers'. They have a range of publications covering all aspects of head injury: what happens, the possible effects and consequences. As will have been noted so far, I have made several references to certain Headway publications and, of course, since they have been written by experts in their fields they can supply much more information on certain issues than I.

They can also provide a list of rehabilitation units specializing in head injury and a list of solicitors who deal with litigation following accidents. Because of their close working relationships with other head injury organizations, they are able to offer a wide range of expertise in many fields and for all age groups. They also offer carers' support groups, day care centres, respite care, activities and therapeutic facilities for those with head injury. (Contacts, postal addresses, telephone numbers and website addresses are included in the Useful Addresses section.)

Carers UK

Carers UK provides carers with help from a variety of angles. The CarersLine (0808 808 7777) responds to over 20,000 enquiries per year and offers free advice and support for carers – from putting them in touch with other organizations and professionals who can help to giving details of state benefits they may be entitled to claim. Carers UK also publish their own magazine, *Caring*, which comes out six times a year and keeps members up to date with the latest news and issues. The organization is committed to raising awareness at all levels of government and society of the needs of carers and ensuring action is taken to support them. They campaigned for the Carers Act 1995, giving carers legal recognition; for the Carers and Disabled Children Act (England and Wales) 2000, giving carers access to services; and are campaigning for the National Strategy for Carers to be implemented.

All this is done through offices in Scotland, Northern Ireland, Wales and England. According to their research, in the UK alone there are nearly 7 million carers which means that one in seven adults care for a relative or friend who are unable to cope alone because of sickness, disability or age. Carers UK realize that these carers need recognition, financial assistance, time off, support services and understanding. With all this help available, I would say that this is an organization that all carers should be in touch with as soon as possible.

The Association to Aid the Sexual and Personal Relationships of People with a Disability (SPOD)

As I stated in Chapter 7, I am not an expert in this field and since any sexual difficulties of the sufferer will not become apparent until they return home, only then will SPOD be mentioned (possibly by the rehabilitation unit) to the carer, as a source of help, and then contact made. I will summarize some of the details they provide in their information booklet.

SPOD is a UK charity dedicated to raising awareness and advancing the rights to equal choice of disabled people in their sexual and personal relationships. The organization provides advice, education, counselling and, where appropriate, treatment. It works closely with its members to ensure it represents their views and makes sure that disabled people's rights and needs are listened to when policies and guidelines that will affect them are implemented by organizations and statutory bodies.

One of SPOD's objectives is, as stated in the information booklet, that they recognize 'the central importance of the social model of disability whilst also acknowledging that professionals have therapeutic and medical expertise that can be invaluable in ensuring disabled people are enabled to make informed and free choices in their personal and sexual relationships'. It also believes that people should experience no restriction or be at any disadvantage in the sexual/personal relationships and choices they make just because they are disabled and may need extra help in carrying out those relationships and choices. In order to meet these aims and objectives SPOD:

- provides a confidential telephone counselling and information service

- publishes material that offers clear, unbiased information

- provides training, awareness-raising talks and seminars for professionals and other interested groups

- contributes to public debate.

These are only some of its roles in this area but to know more, I suggest they be contacted at the address given under the section of Useful Addresses at the end of the book.

Returning to work

This is the last but by no means the least important of what I hope will prove to be useful information for sufferers who like me were the principal source of income in their households. The ability to provide for and protect their family is for most parents a top priority. This is often bound up with one's sense of a role in life, one's self-worth and value to the family. For me personally, as a man, husband and father, I felt that it was my role to earn money and provide for my family. Often, however, for the brain injured this desire to get back to work and start providing for their family is not always easily fulfilled so let me relate what steps I took to get there, the problems I faced along the way and the way I dealt with them.

Unfortunately, there are two questions which present themselves when the sufferer either feels well enough or desirous of returning to work (those two situations not necessarily coinciding). First, they may already be well enough aware of their situation, health condition and what abilities (physical or mental) they may have lost. However, they may not know what their working abilities and stamina levels are and what may be required in relation to any specific occupation, which raises the second problem, what occupation should they pursue?

As I outlined in Chapter 9, when I was first preparing to be discharged from Rosehill, Penny Weekes, one of the OTs, told me I had a unique opportunity which didn't often come to men of my age – that of taking up a new career. I was of course strongly dissuaded by Pauline, Rosehill and my GP from returning to window cleaning, for obvious reasons, though strangely enough even now I have no real fear of going back to it. So my former occupation was out of the question. As I could not yet drive due to my epilepsy and my stamina and perception levels were very low, I could not take up what would have been my next chosen occupation, commercial salesmanship. So the next question was, what form of employment could I realistically take up and how could I find out what was suitable for me?

My first step was through my local employment office where I was put in contact with a Disability Employment Advisor (DEA). Here I learned that my first hurdle was, since I was on certain government benefits, that if I returned to employment of any kind – full- or part-time – I would need to find out how much money I could legally earn and how it would affect my benefits. As it had been my desire and determination right from the outset to return to work but because various problems had made that return difficult or impossible, I'm afraid that at least once each year, usually about January or February when the desire became strongest, I would put the resident DEA through the same procedure. I would often find that the government guidelines had changed, so in a sense the goal posts had moved and there were now new requirements needed to achieve my goal.

Despite being very pleasant people and proficient in their job, DEAs were usually very knowledgeable in dealing with physically disabled people but their knowledge and understanding of brain injury seemed to be inadequate. This is a flaw not of their making but, as pointed out earlier in this chapter, of the system. Finally I suggested to Rosehill that all local DEAs be invited to a presentation on brain injury. This was the same presentation that took place at Torbay Hospital in Torquay on 14 June 2000 (see Chapter Nine).

Unfortunately, I found that it was often more profitable to stay on benefits than to try and do some form of work. However, I didn't take advantage of this situation, partly because of my principles (which for me come from my religious beliefs) and partly because of my deep desire to get back to providing for my family.

I found during my discussions with a DEA that there was a benefit available to disabled people called therapeutic earnings: earnings which, as the name suggests, were available for any kind of employment considered by one's GP and DSS adjudicator to be of therapeutic benefit to the sufferer. On that basis, I approached the DSS with my writing as a form of employment and my GP agreed that, therapeutically for my brain, writing would be beneficial. However, my suggestion failed to meet the requirements because I had suggested it and not my GP and I would not be actually employed by anyone but would be freelance, so I didn't qualify, but more on that later.

The one thing that my DEA did do was to help me become installed in a government scheme called 'Training in Work'. What I had to do was approach an employer who would be willing to take me on for a ten week period (unpaid) and then put them in touch with my DEA who would then check out my goals and follow my progress on a daily and weekly basis.

I did two sessions with two different employers and learned the answers to many of my questions. I didn't know, due to my stamina levels, how many hours each week I would be able to work. I had not worked with anyone, one-to-one (such as in an office environment), for going on 22 years because I had been self-employed, and now because of the brain damage, I had trouble at times mixing with and relating to people, so I wondered whether I would now be able to cope. If the only work available was repetitive, could I manage, and since I now really had a desire to work in an office, was I mentally capable of doing such work?

It was clear that without the answers to these questions, I would never know just what forms of employment to apply for. Then, in 2000, my new DEA made me aware of a new government initiative called 'New Deal', designed to help, amongst others, disabled and the long-term sick to get back to work. Locally a factory unit had been set up where various types of work – repetitive, office, mechanical engineering and warehousing – were available for a number of people who were disabled, physically or mentally. A six week programme was set up for me there, with the goal of determining the answers to the above questions.

Having found what I was best suited for, I was at the end of the period to approach the company I had already completed the ten week 'Training in Work' session with. As it happened I knew them quite well since I used to do business with them when I sold commercial catering equipment before the accident. They gave me part-time employment (half a day a week) selling domestic electrical equipment in their showroom. I was then able to apply and qualify for therapeutic earnings which meant I could earn up to £20 a week without it affecting my benefits.

One final piece of advice: when approaching a prospective employer, don't give them a list of all the problems that you have as unfortunately it can frighten some people off as I found out to my cost in the early days. Just explain the main problems that may or may not affect them, e.g. epilepsy, deafness, needs for regular breaks etc. They deserve to know this but don't need to know all the intricate details.

It took me seven years to reach my goal of getting back to work, albeit only part-time, but I proved to myself that with determination I was able to achieve my target and also proved that anyone else could do the same if they were determined and had the encouragement of family, friends, carers and others.

Chapter 12

What of the Future?

Some Hopes and Aspirations

Having read thus far some may feel what hopes and aspirations can carers and sufferers possibly have, realistically? I have divided this subject up under four headings, though there may well or should be others.

Continuing to be positive

Even if it has not yet been experienced by those involved, I think I have clearly shown that being positive is not always going to be easy and being negative, on the part of sufferers and carers alike, may be a lot easier. Sufferers, of course, may feel they have plenty of reasons to be negative. Physically and mentally they are now limited in many ways, e.g. working, driving and operating certain electrical or electronic equipment. Their marriage, family relationships and some friendships may not be the same as they were.

Carers, especially if they are related to the sufferer, may also feel they have many reasons to be negative. They may feel they have not only lost a loved partner, a beloved parent or child or a close friend, but that they now have much more work to do in caring for the sufferer and family, besides having to provide for their material needs. So their loss has created more work for them and perhaps left an emotional vacuum too. Therefore, whilst on all sides negativity is easy to understand and appreciate, it must not be allowed to take over. On the part of sufferers, a negative attitude may slow down if not totally prevent any progress being made (as already discussed in Chapter 4, recovery made by sufferers often will depend much on their own attitude and frame of mind) and negativity could also make them miserable and unpleasant for other people to want to be around. On the part of carers, it could prevent them encouraging and helping sufferers to progress.

So how can sufferers remain positive, despite all their apparent drawbacks? One way is to, first, consider and appreciate the fact that they are at least still alive, second that they have loving and caring relatives and friends and third, the making of and attaining of goals.

Continuing to make goals

My family and many of my friends have often heard me quote my favourite Chinese proverb, 'a journey of a thousand miles begins with a single step'. The moral clearly is that to reach any goal, one has to first begin somewhere and then keep going. It is this principle which has helped to keep me going forward for the past seven years.

It was the aim the OTs at Rosehill set me right from the beginning of my rehabilitation – they first helped me see the benefit of making goals, no matter how small, and then reaching for and attaining them. Once I had grasped the feeling of achievement, they then began to help me set new goals and then at the reviews which I had every six weeks, the team would ask me what goals I would like to try and achieve by the next review. By looking at copies of those reviews, which I still have, I see that I had the following aims and achievements:

Date	Aims
21/3/95 *First day at Rosehill*	• Assess deficits in attention, memory and judgement. • Rehearse daily living skills, e.g. dressing, safety in kitchen. • Raise self-esteem. • Provide education and support for family.
18/7/95	• To walk independently. • To improve judgement in time keeping.
18/10/95	• Rehearse walking in the community. • Work on numeracy, time estimation and judgement. • Upgrade cooking sessions. • Teach coping strategies of walking outside and in crowds and staying alone at home.
18/1/96	• Complete independence in the community including road safety as a pedestrian. • Assess use of public transport.

	• Complete kitchen assessments unsupervised. • Set up routine of cooking at home. • Set up card system for timing and temperatures in kitchen. • To become more aware of need to control own fatigue. • Continue physiotherapy sessions three times per week. • Provide exercise regime for home use. • Reduce weight to 13 stone. • Liaise with DEAs.
16/4/96 *Last day at Rosehill*	(No aims recorded.)
22/7/97 *First year follow-up*	• Seizures less frequent so reduced anxiety in family giving patient more confidence to be on own at home and out and about. • Also improvement in time management.

After leaving Rosehill, with the OTs Penny Weekes and Mandy McVitie.

These are only some of the main aims I set for myself. By this time I was cooking on my own, walking into town on my own, had begun public speaking again, my time telling was more or less back to normal (except following a seizure). All this, as well as having my first article published, raised my self-esteem tremendously. I had used public transport for the first time on my own and was now using certain electrical equipment unsupervised.

These as well as many other things had begun to make life seem worth living again. However, although certain areas had improved, I see from the review of 22 July 1997 that my irritability level had increased, I was still having problems with certain areas of social intercourse and was not coping very well with the fact that I was not yet ready for work. When I look back at these reviews and consider where I am today, I find it hard to believe that I have got this far and yet I don't feel that I have quite achieved my full potential. I say all this to show that the setting of goals must never be underestimated.

For Rosehill, my setting these goals and achieving them was not their only objective – they showed me how to achieve them and along the way supported and encouraged me, giving me commendation where appropriate, thus building my confidence and self-esteem. From this can be seen the need for all to remain positive. If Rosehill had not been positive, then their beds would still be full of people who had been there for years without ever progressing and Rosehill's ultimate goal with everyone, where practical, was to help them return home.

One thing that everyone needs to be aware of, and that the OTs at Rosehill stressed with me, is the need to be realistic about the goals we set and to do that, one has to be aware of their limitations.

Being realistic of one's abilities and hopes

At times I would forget I had limitations and could no longer do what I used to and then the OTs would remind me to be realistic in my expectations and of my abilities. For example, as highlighted in the last chapter, my goal from the outset was to get back to work and my hope was to work full-time but as time went along and I became more aware of my limitations, so my goal had to change. I came to realize that working full-time was beyond my abilities but my goal to work did not change so I realistically accepted I could only work part-time.

So although sufferers will have to come to terms with having limitations, whatever they may be, this does not prevent them from still making goals and striving for them but they must be realistic and accept that there are or may be certain things they will never be able to do. In this, carers have a large part to play. They of course, especially if they are related to the sufferer, will wish them to be back as they were but will also have to come to the same realization.

Therefore, whilst remaining positive carers will need to sit down with the sufferer and discuss their goals and, without ridiculing or simply pouring cold water on the idea, ask if they think it is within their capabilities. Of course, this will not be easy to do without causing upsets and disagreements but is vital for the sufferer's self-esteem. They may already have a low opinion of themselves, so if they constantly make goals for them-selves and then fail to achieve them or if they are simply slapped down or ridiculed, then their plunge into depression may not be very far away and is to be avoided at all costs. So both sufferers and carers will need to learn to be realistic in the goals that are set if progress is to be made towards getting back to some sort of normality.

Getting back to an average life

An average life for either carer or sufferer may seem as unlikely as flying to the moon but I hope that I have made it clear that although life as it was may not be possible, an average life under the circumstances that now prevail must not be ruled out.

Social life

Carers and sufferers alike may feel that a social life is out of the question, whether that be with their old friends or a new social circle. The carer especially may worry either how or even whether those in their care will fit in socially and whether others will treat them with understanding or instead shun them or treat them as an oddity.

Much will depend on three main factors, how the sufferer behaves, how they perceive themselves and how others perceive them. As we have already seen, the answers to those factors are very much unknown but the carer might be able to do something to help, especially in a known social circle. They could, without appearing to be overprotective, explain the facts and the situation, bearing in mind that there will probably be much ignorance even among friends.

And one thing which overrides all these things and which both carers and sufferers must remember is that if they avoid mixing socially with those not in the same situation as themselves, their circle of friends will be very small, their number of social activities very limited and they may well become insular and introvert. They must accept that because of what has happened to them, they cannot totally avoid an occasional jarring with their contacts in life.

Marriage

If the sufferer is single, of marriageable age and considering marriage, they may come to what I personally feel is not a necessary conclusion – that they can only marry someone who is also a sufferer. They may assume that a non-sufferer would not be interested in them because of their condition or feel they could not cope with the enormity of such a task. As with any marriage, sufferers have the right to a freedom of choice of who they marry – whether that be a sufferer or a non-sufferer. However, I would always advise that the sufferer talk it over first with their carer, a close friend or the rehabilitation unit.

Parenthood

Some sufferers avoid parenthood at all costs because they are afraid of passing on their infirmity to their offspring. However, as with most ailments, unless it is congenital and/or runs in the family, brain injury cannot be passed on by birth.

Perhaps the only things that sufferers need be concerned with in making a decision about whether to have children or not are these: do they feel that, considering their health and circumstances, they can care for, provide for and cope with bringing up a child? How will they feel when their child's friends find out that their parents have brain injury? Do they feel it would be fair or wise to have a child who might possibly become partly responsible for caring for a brain injured parent, especially as the parent ages? These are not meant to be negatives but are practical and realistic considerations to be borne in mind before bringing another life into the world.

Summary

At the risk of repeating myself, let me remind carers and sufferers that being stricken with brain injury does not mean that many normal activities of life need end, in fact it is vital, where possible, that they be continued so that the carer and sufferer's future can be filled with hopes and aspirations.

In Conclusion

Possibly next to ourselves or a loved one being diagnosed as having an incurable illness or losing someone close in death, I personally can think of nothing worse that can happen to someone than having brain injury. The result is rather like having a person physically but not quite mentally present.

Writing this book has for me been an enlightening experience. It has helped me think on some things which I have either not thought about before or at least not thought about for quite some time. With other things, it has made me question them so that I now better understand them and realize I had been taking them for granted.

Learning to live with brain injury really involves learning a whole new way of life for the carer and sufferer. The best way I can describe it is that it is rather like being given a whole new book full of blank pages and being told to fill them, the result being a brand-new life. At first glance, that's a very scary, daunting prospect but I and others like me have proved it can be done just so long as it is remembered that where there is life there is hope and there is definitely life after brain injury.

References

Appleton, R. and Baldwin, T. (eds) (1998) *Management of Brain-Injured Children.* Oxford: Oxford University Press.

Awake! (2000) 'Sleep Is Not a Luxury.' *Awake!*, 8 May 2001, p.28.

Awake! (2001) 'Use Your Brain.' *Awake!*, 22 May 2001, p.25.

Department of Health (2002) 'Hospital In-Patient Data.' *www.doh.gov.uk*

Gorman, C. (2000) 'We Love Fish.' *Time*, 30 October 2000, p.92.

Headway – the brain injury association (2002) 'The Human Brain.' 'Consequences of Traumatic Brain Injury.' *www.headway.org.uk*

Holford, K. (1996) *Activities for the Head Injured at Home.* Nottingham: Headway.

Kreuter, M., Dahllöf, A.G., Gudjonsson, G., Sullivan, M. and Siösteen, A. (1998) 'Sexual Adjustment and Its

Predictors after Traumatic Brain Injury.' *Brain Injury* *12,* 5, 349–368.

McMillan, T. and Greenwood, R. (1991) *Rehabilitation Programmes for the Brain Injured Adult: Current Practice and Future Options in the UK.* A Discussion Paper for the Department of Health, London.

New York Times (2000) 'A Decade of Discovery Yields a Shock about the Brain.' *New York Times*, 4 January 2000.

Further Reading

Gronwall, D.M.A., Wrightson, P. and Waddell, P. (1998) *Head Injury: The Facts: A Guide for Families and Care-Givers.* 2nd edition. Oxford: Oxford University Press.

Powell, T. (1994) *Head Injury – A Practical Guide.* Bicester: Speechmark Publishing/Winslow Press and Headway.

Useful Addresses

Brain Injury Association (USA)
105 North Alfred Street
Alexandria
Virginia 22314
USA
Tel: 703 236 6000; Fax: 703 236 6001
Help Line: 1 800 444 6443
www.biausa.org

British Association of Brain Injury Case Managers
PO Box 1919
Sheffield S7 2DW
Tel: 0700 222 2426

British Epilepsy Association
New Anstey House
Gate Way Drive
Yeadon
Leeds LS19 7XY
Tel: 0113 210 8800; Fax: 0113 391 0300
Freephone Help Line: 0808 800 5050
e-mail: *epilepsy@bea.org.uk; www.epilepsy.org.uk*

British Injury Rehabilitation Trust (BIRT)
First Floor
32 Market Place
Burgess Hill
West Sussex RH15 9WP
Tel: 0144 425 8377; Fax: 0144 423 9123
e-mail: *birt@disabilities-trust.org.uk*; *www.birt.co.uk*

Carers UK
Ruth Pitter House
20/25 Glasshouse Yard
London EC14 4JT
Tel: 020 7490 8818; Fax: 020 7490 8824
CarersLine: 0808 808 7777
e-mail: *info@ukcarers.org.uk*; *www.carersonline.org.uk*

Disabled Living Foundation (DLF)
380–384 Harrow Road
London W9 2HU
Tel: 020 7289 6111; Help Line: 0845 130 9177
e-mail: *info@dlf.org.uk*; *www.dlf.org.uk*

Headway – the brain injury association
4 King Edward Court
King Edward Street
Nottingham NG1 1EW
Tel: 0115 924 0800; Information Line: 0115 947 1919
Fax: 0115 958 4446
e-mail: *information@ headway.org.uk*; *www.headway.org.uk*

International Brain Injury Association
505 Wythe Street
Alexandria Virginia 22314
USA
Tel: 701 683 8400; Fax: 703 683 8996
e-mail: *info@internationalbrain.org*; *www.internationalbrain.org*

Leonard Cheshire Foundation
National Information Officer
30 Millbank
London SW1P 4QD
Tel: 020 7802 8200; Fax: 020 7802 8250
e-mail: *info@london.leonard-cheshire.org.uk*; *www.lcf.org.uk*

The Association to Aid the Sexual and Personal Relationships of People with a Disability (SPOD)
286 Camden Road
London N7 0BJ
Tel: 020 7607 8851; Fax: 020 7700 0236
e-mail: *spoduk@aol.com*; *www.spod-uk.org*